GUITAR MASTERY

A Complete Guide: Basics to Virtuoso in Ten Easy Steps

MUSIC MASTERY SERIES, VOLUME 2

I0520249

By Tad Sisler

To my beautiful, talented sister Kathleen,
who instilled in me a deep love for the guitar
at a very young age.

TABLE OF CONTENTS: PAGE

FOREWORD

I t is ironic that I am writing this book. I have always been a piano/keyboard player and vocalist by trade. My love affair with the guitar has been huge since childhood. Still, my mother **Elaine** was a concert pianist, so she instilled a greater love, perhaps, of the piano in me at a very early age.

Tad's Mother — Elaine Witt Sisler at Age 16
Source — Sisler Private Collection

Throughout my illustrious career spanning over fifty years as a performer, producer, composer, and editor, I've been fortunate to collaborate with numerous guitar virtuosos. This book, however, was born from my experiences in the recording studios as a producer/editor and the countless gigs I've shared with guitar players of all calibres, each bringing their unique magic to the stage.

As my journey in the music industry progressed, I witnessed the thrilling evolution from producing in the traditional 2-inch 24-track tape-based studios to the advent of computer midi music and digital recording. This transition opened doors for me to record guitarists who were not just skilled, but truly exceptional, and others who were, without a doubt, the finest players on the planet. It was my responsibility to enhance their sound, a challenge I embraced with enthusiasm.

As studio recording evolved from outboard effects to plug-ins, it helped to have the history of understanding a cross-fade, for instance, being based upon the old tape splicing that we did back in the day or all the nuances in sounds from vintage amps to modern effects. It is essential to stay current in your knowledge of instruments, hardware, and software, especially in this fast-changing new world of AI. But, mostly, the most important thing you can do is to learn your instrument from top to bottom, and you'll be able to easily transition into any new developments with your developed knowledge and expertise.

I had a ten-year gig as a music developer with **Yamaha Corporation of America**, copying thousands of iconic recordings note-for-note through midi recording and audio conversion, learning to emulate whatever instrument was on the original recording and duplicate the sound. This experience gave me a profound knowledge of guitars, amps, and effects throughout modern history.

Today, I actually "farm out" most of my guitar track needs to the best guitarists in the world. These virtuosos prefer to record using their own setups. Accepting the Pro Tools files back completed sure beats the hours I spent at the console recording a guitarist repeatedly to get the desired tracks.

As an author, I recently won a coveted **Reader's Favorite Award** for a biography I wrote on the life of a famous trumpeter.

Everybody has a different reason for picking up the guitar. Maybe you want to impress your peers or the opposite sex. Perhaps you want to find a vehicle for the talent you know lies within you. Maybe you want to make money or have fame. Whatever motivates you to learn should stay at the forefront as you go through moments of frustration and grow. My old friend **Trini Lopez** was a great guitarist and singer with enormous fame. He had a string of #1 Hits and was invited to the White House to sing for **President John F. Kennedy** as a very young man. **Trini's** motivation in the beginning was to provide for his family. **Trini** said:

"I've had an ambition to be somebody since I was thirteen years old because I wanted to help my family. I wanted to hurry and grow up so I could make enough money to buy my father a big car and my mother a beautiful home with an electric washing machine and all those things she used to see in the newspapers."

Tad Sisler with Trini Lopez
Source – Sisler Private Collection

Making mistakes while learning is okay if you pick yourself up, dust yourself off, and move on. It's all about growing. I have a running gag with my friends. Whenever we make a mistake while performing, we call it "improvisation!" Guitar blues legend **B.B. King** said:

"Playing the guitar is like telling the truth. You can't hide your mistakes, and you can't hide your soul."

I still produce many great guitarists in my studio, virtuosos who play classical nylon string or high-end modern jazz and don't have the studio chops (or just want to play and not mess with the recording aspect), and the playing is so good it's a pleasure to work through it with them even still.

So, how did I come around to writing this book? Over many years of experience and curiosity working with the greats, I asked many questions. I researched how to do it right from the ground up. This book will emphasize the practical and creative aspects of learning guitar, and much of it comes through the eyes of legendary players who have come up through the ranks in their unique way. It's easier to find the light at the end of the tunnel when you've been through it a few times. And, if you play guitar or piano, you don't need to rely on others to work. A drummer only sounds as good as the band he is backing. A guitarist can do an amazing solo. Even the biggest stars get great pleasure from solo performances, like **Ed Sheeran, John Mayer** and **Taylor Swift**.

"The guitar is like a good woman. Touch her in the right place in the right way and she will move you in ways you never dreamed about."
— Rod Stewart

Tad Sisler with Rod Stewart
Source – Sisler Private Collection

I could be a better guitar player. I play "at" the guitar. But I know how to make a guitar sound great, and I can tell... in my sleep... an excellent performance from a bad one. My friend **Tony Robbins**, the great motivator, always suggests that if you want to excel at anything, look at who is doing it well and do that!

I hope you are now or will become the best player on the planet. I can attest to having been in the same studio or stage with players who made me a better performer through their expertise and excellence. Through your journey, I hope this book helps you to have an extraordinary career or at least a better understanding of how the guitar works and how to get the most out of it.

INTRODUCTION
ARTIST SPOTLIGHT
ERIC CLAPTON

"The guitar is the coolest instrument in the world. It's got everything: melodic possibilities, harmonic possibilities, it's incredibly rhythmic."
– Eric Clapton

Eric **Clapton**, legendary guitarist in rock and blues history, began his musical journey from humble beginnings. Born in 1945 and raised by his grandparents in Ripley, Surrey, England, **Clapton** faced emotional struggles early in life, initially believing his mother was his sister.

At the age of 13, **Clapton** was gifted his first guitar, a modest *Hoyer* steel-stringed acoustic, which was challenging to play. Initially, the learning curve was steep, and it took him a while to produce a sound. But, his resolve was unyielding. **Clapton** was self-taught, immersing himself in records and painstakingly attempting to replicate the sounds he heard. His musical influences were the blues greats like **Robert Johnson, Muddy Waters**, and **B.B. King,** whose styles deeply resonated with him.

I can relate to this because, as a teenager, I lost myself in playing my instruments and singing, listening to and emulating all the artists of my time. My music helped me through my difficult teen years.

Clapton's dedication was unwavering. He spent hours each day practicing, developing his style. He would slow down records to understand the nuances of each note and chord, refining his technique with relentless practice. His persistence paid off, and he soon became known for his exceptional skill and emotional depth in playing the guitar.

Clapton's talent soon garnered attention. He became a member of **The Yardbirds** and later **John Mayall & the Bluesbreakers**, cementing his status. His global recognition skyrocketed with the establishment of **Cream** in 1966. I remember as a kid seeing that **Cream** filled huge stadiums all over the world, and it was just three musicians on stage! Even though he had personal demons, **Clapton's** commitment to music remained strong because of his unwavering dedication.

Today, the world celebrates **Eric Clapton** as one of the greatest guitarists ever. His journey from a struggling beginner to a legendary virtuoso inspires us all. His story shows how perseverance and passion can lead to extraordinary success.

In emphasizing the versatility of the guitar, Eric Clapton encourages players to explore all the guitar's capabilities.

Eric Clapton
Source – Wikimedia Commons

In crafting this book, I will guide you on a transformative journey, starting from your current level of guitar proficiency and leading you toward virtuosity, even if you've never strummed a chord. We'll delve into the wisdom of the legends who paved the way, like **Eric Clapton**, and together, we'll uncover the universal struggles, fears, and initial challenges that accompany any worthwhile learning process.

This book will explore and cultivate all the essentials of becoming a great guitarist. Whether you're a beginner or just looking to improve skills that are already strong, this guide will equip you with techniques, knowledge, and the mindset you will need to unlock your full potential as a guitar player.

Much of the information here may seem highly elementary if you're an advanced player. Still, the best way to teach is to start at the very beginning... the idea is to go back to the fundamentals that make you an extraordinary musician.

Much of the knowledge and theory outlined in this book crosses over to learning any instrument, although it's all aimed at the guitarist.

This book addresses skill development, confidence building, creative expression, and every other element that separates the good players from the great ones.

SELF-DISCIPLINE

Many people have told me, *"I always wanted to learn how to play guitar, but I have no self-discipline."* Self-discipline is not something you have or don't have. It's something you make happen. Whether you're a religious person or not, you can understand the concept that when God created us, we were given this amazing power to choose, a power so strong that we actually can use it to choose against God if we want to.

I understand the power of addictions, but we can choose to overcome smoking or drugs, or anything we put our minds to. Self-discipline is your choice. You can become the best at what you do if you decide that there is no other option but success. This all starts with self-discipline, with your choice to make it happen, and then to persist until you've succeeded. It's that simple. If you don't believe you can learn an instrument, you probably won't. But I promise you, if you follow the wisdom and resources of this book, you will find your way if you stick with it.

The journey of learning and growth is all about determination, a positive attitude, and a strong willingness to embrace advice and criticism. As you progress, remember the wise words of my old friend, **President George H.W. Bush**, who compiled a list of thoughts to guide us along our path:

"1. Don't get down when your life takes a bad turn. Out of adversity comes challenge and often success.
2. Don't blame others for your setbacks.
3. When things go well, always give credit to others.
4. Don't talk all the time. Listen to your friends and mentors and learn from them.
5. Don't brag about yourself. Let others point out your virtues, your strong points.
6. Give someone else a hand. When a friend is hurting, show that friend you care.
7. Nobody likes an overbearing big shot.

8. As you succeed, be kind to people. Thank those who help you along the way.
9. Don't be afraid to shed a tear when your heart is broken because a friend is hurting.
10. Say your prayers!!"

Tad with President George H.W. Bush and Barbara Bush
Source – Sisler Private Collection

So, join me on this transformative journey as we DIVE INTO UNLEASHING YOUR **GUITAR GOD** WITHIN and discover the potential within you to master the guitar!

Medical Disclaimer:

CHAPTER ONE
THE JOURNEY BEGINS
EMBRACING THE GUITAR

"I'm only myself when I have a guitar in my hands." — George Harrison

Guitar playing has become a global phenomenon, with an estimated **410 million people** playing the guitar worldwide. This remarkable number highlights the instrument's widespread appeal and enduring popularity across most cultures and age groups. Online learning platforms and resources rose during the COVID-19 pandemic, significantly contributing to this surge, making it easier for people to pick up the guitar as a new hobby.

Additionally, countries like India are emerging as significant markets, with over **10 million guitar players** and a growth rate of approximately 15% per year in acoustic guitar sales. References – Guitar Mammoth and Breakthrough Guitar

These statistics underscore the guitar's role not just as a musical instrument but as a cultural icon and a source of emotional comfort and creativity for millions of people around the globe.

Several years back, I read an article about a study by a local college in **New York City**. A young man would randomly approach young women and ask for their phone number for a date. Then, the very same young man dressed the same way, now with a guitar strapped to his back, would go up to young women and ask for their phone number for a date. Surprisingly, many more young women were willing to go out with the young man when he had a guitar strapped to his back, never even knowing if he could play! So, there is power in the instrument beyond what we even know!

Now, let's delve into the ten easy steps I've promised you in the title. This guide, born out of a wealth of life experiences and countless sessions with master guitarists, is designed to empower you on your journey toward guitar mastery. Each step is a steppingstone toward your musical potential and much more:

- **Choose the Right Guitar**
- **Learn Basic Guitar Anatomy**
- **Tune Your Guitar**
- **Practice Proper Posture**
- **Learn Basic Chords**
- **Practice Strumming Patterns**
- **Play Simple Songs**
- **Use a Metronome**
- **Develop Finger Strength and Dexterity**
- **Play Regularly and Stay Consistent**

Looking at all ten steps at once can be daunting for a beginner, but just remember what my friend, the great actor **Robert Wagner** said:

> *"I've learned one important thing about God's gifts — what we do with them is our gift to him."*

Make this your mission, to develop your talents and share your gift with the world.

Robert Wagner and Tad Sisler
Source – Sisler Private Collection

CHOOSING THE RIGHT GUITAR: The first step is choosing the right guitar, an important factor to consider primarily based on your music preference. As you get more proficient, you'll move to different guitars and styles, and that's part of the fun.

HISTORY OF THE GUITAR: Before we get into what guitar you should choose, let's look at a brief history of how the guitar evolved:

Historians believe the guitar is born from the lute, a stringed instrument dating back to around 3100 B.C. in the Middle East. The lute was generally a plucked or bowed instrument.

No one knows where the first guitar originated, but history scholars assume that the first guitars came from Spain. The *Guitarra Latina* was a stringed instrument and the precursor to the modern guitar during medieval times. It had a deeper body and a narrower neck than today's guitars.

Early guitars from the 16th century generally had four strings, tuned in C-F-A-D. The belly of the guitar was the soundboard with a circular hole created to amplify the sound of the strings through the deep-bodied belly.

A **"bridge"** was built onto the far end of the belly, guiding the strings to the pegbox on the neck. The pegbox on the end of the neck was modelled after the violin, anchoring the strings on the end.

Modern guitars are much like the early guitars in shape. Still, the guitar has evolved in a hundred different ways since the early guitar was born.

Unless you're playing a modified guitar, odds are yours will have six strings, tuned in E -A – D – G – B – E.

TYPES OF GUITARS IN TODAYS MARKETPLACE

Many different types of guitars exist today. Here are the basics, and if you're not familiar with some of the features or terminology of each, we'll get into the anatomy of the guitar as we delve further into this book.

ACOUSTIC GUITAR: Hollow-bodied instruments with steel strings, acoustic guitars produce sound through the vibration of the strings, resonating in the chamber of the body, offering a natural, warm tone, and popular in singer-songwriter, folk, country, and acoustic rock genres. Successful artists with acoustic guitar mastery who left a significant mark on music history include **Joni Mitchell, Bob Dylan, Joan Baez**, and **James Taylor.**

CLASSICAL GUITAR: With a broader neck and nylon strings, the classical guitar is softer and mellow, commonly applied in classical, bossa-nova, and flamenco music, allowing for fingerstyle technique in playing.

Masters of the classical guitar include **Andrés Segovia, Julian Bream, and John Williams**.

ELECTRIC GUITAR: Utilizing pick-ups within the instrument and relying upon amplification, electric guitars come in solid-body, hollow-body, and semi-hollow styles, offering a wide range of tones and prevalent in jazz, blues, rock, and many other genres. Artists who made lasting contributions to music with their electric guitar mastery include **Prince, Jimmy Page, Eric Clapton**, and **Terry Kath**.

STRATOCASTER: A trendy guitar featuring a double-cutaway solid body, three single-coil pick-ups, and built-in vibrato, the Strat is a classic model electric guitar known for its versatility and a favorite of iconic guitarists worldwide. Iconic performers who chose the Stratocaster as a primary instrument include **Jimi Hendrix, Jeff Beck, David Gilmour**, and **Mark Knopfler**.

"Music is my religion. I could die for it. I could die for you. My beliefs about music are completely spiritual. I think it's the highest form of communication in existence." – Jimi Hendrix

Jimi Hendrix
Credit: Wikimedia Commons

LES PAUL: With a single-cutaway solid body and two humbucking pickups, the **Les Paul** generates a warm, thick tone. Widely used in blues, jazz, and rock genres. Other than the creator of this guitar himself, great artists who chose a **Les Paul** guitar as a primary instrument include **Slash** and **Joe Perry**.

Les Paul changed music with his revolutionary "New Sound". He was the pioneer of complex multi-track recordings on acetate discs, layering his guitar parts and adjusting the speed of the tape recorder to create effects. **Bing Crosby** gifted **Les Paul** an *Ampex* reel-to-reel tape recorder, allowing him to achieve even more sophisticated sound-on-sound recording. His signature guitar is not the only device he used to change the world of guitar playing and recording.

Les Paul
Credit — Flickr/Creativecommons.org

TELECASTER: An instrument featuring a solid body, two single-coil pickups, and a unique bridge, the **Telecaster** is known for its simple, twangy sound. This guitar is super popular with country artists and rock and indie players, including **Keith Richards, Bruce Springsteen,** and **James Burton**.

HOLLOW-BODIED: Popular in blues, rockabilly, and jazz with an expressive, rich sound, these guitars sport an entirely hollow body, usually with a sound hole, offering up resonance and warmth. **B.B. King** loved his hollow-bodied guitar. **George Benson** and **Wes Montgomery** also made magic from this instrument.

TWELVE-STRING: An acoustic model doubling the six strings with another set of octave strings, the **12-string guitar** is the granddaddy of folk and acoustic rock, with a shimmering, rich sound, adding texture and depth to the overall sound of a recording or standing tall and proud on its own. Iconic artists on twelve-string include **Roger McGuinn, Lead Belly,** and **Tom Petty**.

"When you play the 12-string guitar, you spend half your life tuning the instrument and the other half playing it out of tune!" — Pete Seeger

ARCHTOP: An instrument known for its full-bodied warmth, **archtop guitars** feature a curved, arched top and back, usually played with a fingerstyle or plucking technique; popular in swing and jazz music. **Wes Montgomery** also used an archtop. Extraordinary jazz guitarists who excelled on an archtop include **Joe Pass** and **Charlie Christian**.

RESONATOR: Also called a **steel guitar**, but not to be confused with **petal-steel**, featuring a metal **resonator** cone (or cones) rather than a traditional sound hole, **resonator guitars** produce a unique metallic tone, and they are the go-to guitar for slide guitar, bluegrass, and many blues applications. I've used this sound in many underscore applications for film, bringing out an emotional, twangy feeling. Great resonator players include **Taj Mahal, Son House,** and **Bukka White.**

"The blues was like that problem child that you may have in the family. You was a little bit ashamed to let anybody see him, but you loved him. You just didn't know how other people would take it." -B.B. King

B.B. King
Credit: Wikimedia Commons

PEDAL-STEEL (or **Steel Guitar**): Characterized by its horizontal layout, foot pedals, and multiple strings, guitarists most often play a **Pedal-Steel** guitar holding a steel bar rolling across the strings, which, along with the manipulation of the foot pedal, creates smooth, gliding sounds while manipulating the pitch. Masters of **Pedal-Steel** include **Buddy Emmons, Paul Franklin,** and **Lloyd Green.**

BARITONE GUITAR: Tuned lower than a standard guitar and producing a rich, deep tone, the baritone guitar is used in surf rock, metal, and alt-rock, adding a distinctive sonic character. Artists who impacted the art form using baritone guitars include **Duane Eddy, Brian Setzer**, and **Robert Smith.**

BASS: My **MUSIC MASTERY SERIES, VOLUME 5** book tackles the bass guitar and upright bass. It's a good read if you want to excel at this instrument.

The bass guitar and drums create the rhythmic foundation for the band or the track. Typically with four strings, although many bass players prefer a five or six-stringed bass guitar, it sports thick strings and a longer neck than traditional guitars. Styles of this instrument vary hugely from the contrabass style acoustic jazz upright to the slamming rock or funk bass guitar, anchoring tracks and providing pop and excitement or warmth, depending upon the application. Successful and impactful bass players include **Paul McCartney, Jaco Pastorius**, and **Flea (Michael Peter Balzary)**.

We will focus on standard acoustic and electric guitars, and which may be best for you.

PROS AND CONS OF ACOUSTIC VS. ELECTRIC

ACOUSTIC GUITAR PROS:

Portability: Acoustic guitars are easy to carry and play anywhere without additional equipment.

Simplicity: They do not require amps, pedals, or cables, making them straightforward and hassle-free.

Sound Quality: They produce a natural, rich sound ideal for genres like folk, country, and classical.

Beginner-Friendly: Easier for beginners to start with as they focus on basic techniques without the distraction of equipment.

CONS:

Physical Effort: Requires more finger strength to press down the strings, which can be challenging for beginners. Replacing steel strings with nylon strings can help somewhat, as they are easier to press on.

Volume Limitation: Sound is limited to the acoustic projection of the guitar, making it less suitable for large venues without amplification.

Less Versatility: Limited in terms of effects and sound manipulation compared to electric guitars.

ELECTRIC GUITAR PROS:

Versatility: Can produce a wide range of sounds and effects, making them suitable for genres like rock, metal, and jazz.

Playability: Generally easier to play due to lighter strings and lower action, requiring less finger strength.

Amplification: These can be amplified to any volume, making them suitable for live performances and recordings.

Customization: Offers various options for tone and effects through amps and pedals, allowing for a personalized sound.

CONS:

Additional Equipment: Requires an amplifier and often other equipment, which can be costly and less portable.

Setup Complexity: More complex setup and maintenance compared to acoustic guitars.

Learning Curve: Beginners may use various sounds and effects to manage overwhelming. Sources: Guitar World, Sweetwater, Music Strive

"I play guitar because it lets me dream out loud." — Michael Hedges

If you're a beginner, many choose to start with an acoustic guitar. There's virtually no setup; it's easy to maneuver and an excellent tool for learning. Acoustic guitars come in different sizes, so a smaller one works very well for teaching children and small hands in general. Nylon strings are good for learning, but getting comfortable with the pressure needed for steel string playing from the start is a good idea.

If you have a specific genre in mind that you're eager to learn, it's wise to focus on the instrument associated with that genre. This approach will not only align your learning with your musical interests but also enhance your motivation and enjoyment.

FACTORS TO CONSIDER

GENRE OF MUSIC:

Acoustic Guitar: Ideal for genres like folk, country, classical, and singer-songwriter music. Because of its rich, natural tones, acoustic guitars complement these styles well.

Electric Guitar: Suited for rock, metal, jazz, and blues. The ability to use effects pedals and amplifiers gives you many choices for sounds and tonal variations, which are essential in these genres.

DESIRED SOUND AND VERSATILITY:

Acoustic Guitar: Provides a warm, resonant sound perfect for solo performances and unplugged sessions.

It's limited to its natural acoustic tone, which can work for or against you, depending on your needs.

Electric Guitar: Offers greater versatility with various effects and amplification options. So many sounds can be generated, from clean and bright to heavily distorted, making it suitable for experimenting with different musical styles.

BUDGET CONSIDERATIONS:

ACOUSTIC: Generally, a more cost-effective choice for beginners due to lower initial and ongoing costs.

•**Lower Entry Cost:** Acoustic guitars generally have a lower initial cost than electric guitars because they do not require additional equipment. You can find a beginner-level acoustic for $100 to $300.

•**Minimal Additional Equipment:** There's no need for an amplifier, cables, or pedals, which keeps ongoing costs low. Most beginners only need a tuner, picks, and possibly a gig bag or case.

ELECTRIC: Offers more versatility and sound options but comes with higher upfront and maintenance expenses due to the need for additional equipment.

•**Higher Entry Cost:** While beginner electric guitars can also start at around $100, the initial investment is higher when you include necessary accessories. You can find decent quality beginner electric guitar packages between $500-$1,000.00.

•**Amplifier and Accessories:** Electric guitars require an amplifier, costing additional money. Accessories like cables, picks, and pedals can add to the cost.

•**Ongoing Expenses:** Maintenance costs can be higher due to the need for new strings, potential repairs, and upgrades to equipment over time.

PHYSICAL COMFORT AND PLAYABILITY

Acoustic Guitars tend to be bulkier and more complex to play due to larger body sizes and heavier strings, which can be challenging for beginners.

Electric Guitars generally offer greater physical comfort and playability with a smaller body, lighter strings, and lower action, but require additional equipment.

ACOUSTIC GUITARS

•**Larger Body Size:** Acoustic guitars typically have a larger and bulkier body, which can be more cumbersome to hold and play, especially for smaller individuals or younger players.

•**Heavier Gauge Strings:** They often use thicker strings, which require more finger strength to press down, potentially causing discomfort for beginners until calluses develop.

•**Higher Action:** Strings are usually set higher from the fretboard (higher action) than electric guitars, making pressing the strings more challenging and tiring for extended playing sessions.

•**No Need for Additional Gear:** Simplifies the learning process as beginners only need the guitar without worrying about amplifiers or pedals.

ELECTRIC GUITARS

•**Smaller Body Size:** Electric guitars generally have a smaller, lighter body, making them more comfortable to play and more accessible to hold.

•**Lighter Gauge Strings:** They typically use lighter strings, which are easier to press down, reducing finger fatigue and making it more comfortable for beginners.

•**Lower Action:** A guitarist will set the strings on electric guitars closer to the fretboard (lower action), which makes them easier to press down and facilitates faster playing.

•**Versatility with Amplification:** While they require additional equipment like amplifiers, this can also enhance playability by allowing for adjustable volume and various sound effects.

MAINTENANCE AND CARE TIPS

ACOUSTIC GUITARS

•**Humidity Control:** Keep the guitar in an environment with stable humidity (ideally 45-55%) to prevent the wood from cracking or warping.

•**Regular Cleaning:** Wipe down the guitar fretboard, strings, and body with a soft cloth after each use to remove sweat and dirt.

ELECTRIC GUITARS

•**String Replacement:** Change strings regularly, as old strings can affect sound quality and playability. Frequency depends on playing time and conditions.

•**Electronics Check:** Periodically check and clean the electronics, including pickups, switches, and output jacks, to ensure optimal performance.

Don't stress too much on which guitar you choose right away. Remember what guitar great **Stevie Ray Vaughan** said,

"Your sound is in your hands as much as anything. It's the way you pick, and the way you hold the guitar, more than it is the amp or the guitar you use."

Stevie Ray Vaughan
Source – Wikimedia Commons

CHAPTER TWO
NURTURING YOUR GUITAR

Believe it or not, the most important thing you can do over time is to wash your hands before you play your guitar! Oils and dirt on your hands will affect the strings, making them deteriorate faster and harder to play. Wiping down your fretboard after each use will also help keep oil and sediment on your strings to a minimum.

Following hand hygiene, the next best practice is to change your strings regularly. Generally, if you're a daily player, consider changing your strings every month. Of course, the type of music you play, and the quality of the strings can influence this frequency. The joy of hearing your guitar's enhanced sound with fresh strings is a reward in itself!

Just like you would do with your car, regular visits to a technician for preventative maintenance are a wise move. Most professional guitarists follow this practice. A skilled technician will fine-tune your guitar's alignment, check your frets, repair any loose parts, deeply clean and polish your guitar, and change your strings. This comprehensive care ensures your guitar's longevity and optimal performance. The main thing is to play and enjoy it regularly.

"The guitar is a language that speaks directly to the soul, transcending boundaries and uniting people through its timeless melodies."
— Sergio Mendes

Sergio Mendes and Tad Sisler
Source — Sisler Private Collection

CHOOSING THE RIGHT GUITAR, AMPLIFIER, AND ACCESSORIES

Having the right gear is so very important, especially in a crowded gig economy with enormous competition. It all starts with the guitar.

Like playing a ukulele at **Carnegie Hall** in a Metal Band, playing the wrong type of guitar for your style will only cause despair and frustration. Consider the body, kind of wood used, number of frets, and pick-ups when looking for a guitar that matches your playing style or preferences.

Most of my professional guitarist friends have multiple guitars they carry to the gig or recording session because they want the right sound for whatever song or vibe is thrown at them. Whether it's a knowledgeable individual at **Guitar Center, Sam Ash,** or **Sweetwater,** seeking the guidance of a pro when choosing a guitar is a wise move. It's far easier than sifting through the hundreds of options and making a blind choice.

"I never wanted to copy or emulate anyone else. I always wanted to find my own voice and create my own sound. That's what being a true artist is all about." – Eddie Van Halen

Eddie Van Halen
Credit: Wikimedia Commons

Amplifiers can generate the same amount of confusion at first. Do you want a tube amp or a solid-state amp, perhaps? Maybe a digital modelling amp is best. Do you need a Marshall Amp Stack, or will a Fender work fine? Try several amps; consider more than one amp for all applications.

Tube amps generate warm, vintage tones. **Solid-state amps** are more reliable and affordable. **Digital modelling amps** are excellent because they combine amplification with effect simulations. Think about how many watts you need and portability (are you going to a small gig or a concert hall?). What tonal options work best?

Most studio producers bypass the guitar amp entirely in favor of amp-simulating plug-ins, or they run a line out from the amp and mic the amp into the mixing board, later combining the sound with effects, including compression.

Similarly, studio producers may ask you to use your effects for your specific sound or their plug-ins to get there.

Effects Boards and **Pedals are your gateway to a world of sonic exploration.**
They allow you to shape and mold your guitar's sound in myriad ways, from
the ethereal reverb to the gritty distortion, the rhythmic delay to the swirling
chorus. If you're new to this, begin with the essential pedals like overdrive or
distortion, delay, and tremolo, and then let your creativity guide you. Many
top brands offer digital all-in-one effect pedal boards that are perfect for the
studio, giving you the power to tap tempo for the delay, or combine effects for
the perfect solo. The key is to use these tools to find your unique sound, a
sound that is unmistakably yours and can resonate with others.

Carlos Santana's guitar, for instance, has an iconic, original sound that you can
always pick out.

"The guitar is your first wings. It's assigned and designed to unfold your
vision and imagination." – Carlos Santana

Carlos Santana
Credit: Wikimedia Commons

BEST EFFECTS FOR GUITAR

Distortion alters the guitar signal to create a gritty, overdriven sound. Distortion is widespread in rock and metal genres, adding intensity and sustain.

Overdrive simulates the sound of a tube amp peaking or overdriving, creating a warm, crunchy tone often used in blues and classic rock. It's a more subtle form of distortion, really.

Reverb adds ambient space to the guitar signal, mimicking the natural echo in various environments. This gives the sound a sense of depth and atmosphere. Many reverb types, including long hall, room, and plate effects, are used for different applications.

Delay repeats the guitar signal at specified intervals, creating echoes that can range from subtle to pronounced. It is often used in rock, ambient, and experimental music. A long delay can alter and add to a solo, whereas a shorter or slap delay might work better in rhythm guitar. I've instructed my guitarist to set the delay to the tempo or BPM of the song on some recordings, so it lines up perfectly.

Chorus slightly detunes and delays the guitar signal as if multiple guitars are playing simultaneously, adding richness and shimmer to the sound.

Wah-wah sweeps through a range of frequencies, producing a distinctive "wah" sound controlled by the player's foot on a pedal. It is popular in funk and rock.

Flanger mixes the guitar signal with a delayed version of itself, creating a sweeping, jet-like sound that adds texture and movement to the guitar tone.

Phaser: Like a flanger but more subtle, a phaser alters the phase of the guitar signal to create a swirling, whooshing effect. It is often used in psychedelic and classic rock.

Tremolo rapidly modulates the guitar signal's volume, creating a pulsing effect that adds rhythmic variation and dynamic movement.

Compression evens out the dynamic range of the guitar signal, making quiet notes louder and loud notes quieter, resulting in a more consistent and polished sound.

Guitar accessories can enhance your experience as a player, including good guitar cables, a tuner, a strap, a guitar stand, a capo, picks, a case (or gig bag) for protection, and wall cradles to ensure safety when wall-hanging.

How much are you willing to invest? If you have all the money you need, splurge on high-end equipment; if you don't, you'll be surprised at the options available at lower prices. Prioritize your purchases according to your budget.

IMPORTANT CONSIDERATION: Although you're only as good as your weakest link, your instrument is the most important purchase you will make, so if you must cut corners, try to keep as much budget as possible for your instrument.

At the heart of your playing experience is comfort and ease. The shape of the neck, the radius of the fretboard, the scale length, the smoothness of the strings, and the effortless chord structures all contribute to how comfortable a guitar feels in your hands. We understand that these factors are crucial to your playing, and we're here to guide you in making the right choice.

Find a guitar that fits the size of your hands and your playing style. Properly set-up action, smooth fret edges, and a comfortable body shape all make a significant difference in your experience as a performer.

"I believe every guitar player inherently has something unique about their playing. They just have to identify what makes them different and develop it." — Jimmy Page

Jimmy Page
Credit: Wikimedia Commons

Several years ago, I brought a guitar virtuoso into my studio. While my talented friend was here, I asked him to do acoustic picking and strumming. This particular player had his master's degree in Classical Guitar from **USC.**

We weren't planning to do this, so he didn't bring his acoustic, but I had a newly purchased **Martin** acoustic in my studio. He grabbed it, tuned it, and played flawlessly, but I could tell he wasn't enjoying the experience. Afterward, he suggested that I take the guitar to his "dude," a guitar tech in Los Angeles who specializes in smoothing out the action of even the highest-end guitars.

The moral of the story here is that you can spend a ton of money on a great guitar and still need to modify it to enjoy your experience.

Along with finding a mentor or pro friend to help guide you into the right purchase, research, and demo before you buy. Read reviews, watch *YouTube* demos, and listen to audio samples of the gear you're looking at. Try it in person at your local music store; go to gear expos or borrow equipment from friends to get that hands-on experience. Most of my friends, however, are very particular about their instruments, and believe me, you'll get the eye roll when you ask about borrowing anything from a professional.

Legendary broadcaster **Larry King** once said:

"I remind myself every morning: Nothing I say this day will teach me anything. So, if I'm going to learn, I must do it by listening."

Larry King and Tad Sisler
Source – Sisler Personal Collection

Ultimately, the key is to play and listen, ensuring the guitar aligns with your unique playing style and desired sound. Remember, it's your personal preference that should guide your choice.

When it comes to **selecting** gear, are you considering versatility? While it's crucial to have equipment that aligns with your unique musical style, opting for gear that can adapt to various genres or playing scenarios can significantly enhance your musical flexibility. For instance, a guitar with coil-splitting or coil-tapping capabilities can open a world of sonic possibilities, allowing you to explore both single-coil and humbucker tones.

As keyboard players, we have the luxury of simply selecting a different patch to achieve our desired sound. However, with the guitar, it's a different story. The instrument and effects are just tools; how we skilfully combine them allows us to create our unique sound. Effects pedals help!

During the many years I performed at corporate events, other than moving a ton of gear (which I hated) every day, we found ourselves in a million different situations: one night we were an awards big band in a tux; the next night we were a beach band, then we did Motown nights, or a jazz trio, or even Arabian nights and other theme events. Every night called for a different vibe, and it was undoubtedly a challenge for all of us to match the style and sound. Fortunately, I worked with the best guitarists who knew what combination of instruments and effects would get us there on any night...

… which leads me to **quality** and **longevity**: when you invest in the good stuff, you get durability and longevity. My first *Yamaha DX7* keyboard came at a price of almost three grand. I was in a terrible auto accident one night on the way home from the gig. The force of the impact bent the keyboard. I thought the accident destroyed the keyboard, but to my amazement, I plugged it in on the next gig, and it not only worked, but it continued to work for the next fifteen years!

Great guitars are like that; if you maintain them, keep them from extremes of cold and heat, and keep them out of being kicked to the ground from your floor, stand by your burly bass player (I broke up more than one stage fight for that reason).

"Rock and roll music, if you like it, if you feel it, you can't help but move to it. That's what happens to me. I can't help it."
– Keith Richards

Keith Richards
Credit: Wikimedia Commons

Ultimately, your choices in gear come down to **personal preference** and **style**. What works for you may not work for someone else, and that's cool. Trust your instincts and grab gear that excites and inspires you. Don't be afraid to reach beyond yourself and try unconventional setups or explore new sounds. You grow through experimentation and personal expression, leading to your signature sound.

"All I've got is a red guitar, three chords and the truth." – *Bob Dylan*

IMPORTANCE OF A GOOD TUNER: Imagine being in the studio, pouring your heart into a perfect performance, only to realize that one of the strings is slightly out of tune, forcing you to discard the entire track. This is the harsh reality of poor tuning, a situation that can be easily avoided with a good tuner.

More than just technicality, **tuning** is the cornerstone of your musical journey. It's the key that unlocks the full potential of your instrument, allowing you to create the harmonious sounds you envision.

In a nutshell, tuning involves adjusting the pitch of each string to ensure that they are in tune with themselves, producing a pleasant sound, and in the correct musical intervals relative to each other.

There's a joke about a guy who goes to see a solo country guitar player, and he shows up just in time to get a good seat. He watches for an extended time as the guitarist tunes his instrument, tunes it again, and tunes it again for an extended period. Finally, in frustration, the guy goes up to the performer and says, *"No offense, sir, but I once went to see Andrés Segovia at the Kennedy Center, and even he didn't take this long to tune his guitar."* To that, the country performer calmly looked up and said, *"Well, maybe he didn't give a shit."* (Insert laughter here and forgive my language!)

Andrés Segovia
Credit: Wikimedia Commons

"The guitar is a small orchestra. It is polyphonic. Every string is a different color, a different voice." — Andrés Segovia

Remember, the key is not to overdo anything, but to understand the value of regular tuning and maintenance. The best guitarists pause to tune their guitars throughout the gig or session, reaping the benefits of optimal performance and sound quality.

Standard tuning, the most prevalent, involves tuning the strings to the pitches e-a-d-g-b-e, from the thickest, lowest string to the thinnest, highest string. This tuning's versatility is its greatest asset, as it is used in all fake books, song charts, and most instructional materials, enabling a wide range of chords and scales.

Alternative tunings offer other unique tonal possibilities, inspiring new musical ideas, including open d (d-a-d-F#-a-d), drop d (d-a-d-g-b-e), and open g (d-g-d-g-b-d). Many artists, including **Joni Mitchell**, regularly use alternative tunings for different songs, providing characteristic sounds useful for blues, slide guitar, folk, or fingerstyle playing.

Joni Mitchell
Credit – Wikimedia Commons

Ensuring your guitar stays in tune is a multi-faceted process, with one crucial step being the proper installation of your strings. This involves ensuring they have the right amount of tension. Strings naturally lose tension over time and detune, so it's important to check and adjust your tuning regularly. Also, **temperature** and **humidity changes** will expand or contract the wood, affecting the tension of the strings.

Today's guitar **tuners** are miracles. A good-quality **tuner**, including clip-on tuners, smartphone apps, and pedal tuners, is crucial for accurate tuning. Easy to use, they provide visual or audible cues to help you to achieve precise tuning. Invest in a reliable tuner to ensure accuracy.

Change your strings regularly, and when you change them, **stretch** them gently to stabilize tuning. New strings stretch and then settle, causing detuning more frequently at first. Pull on each string and return it several times, accelerating the stretching process and vastly reducing the need for constant re-tuning.

Maintain your guitar for **optimal tuning stability**. Please keep it clean and free of dirt or dust affecting the strings or tuning pegs. Lubricate the bridge saddles and nuts with a good lubricant, reducing friction and improving tuning stability.

Also, be mindful of your **playing technique.** Like the old classic rock piano players who banged hard and jumped on the keys until they trashed the piano, your guitar will go out of tune quicker with heavy-handed guitar playing or excessive bending of the strings. It won't last as long as a valued instrument. Work on a balanced approach to your playing, fretting, and strumming, minimizing unnecessary movement of strings.

"All the world is a birthday cake, so take a piece, but not too much."
— George Harrison

George Harrison
Credit: Wikimedia Commons

Remember always to be bold and **double-check** your **tuning** before and even during playing if necessary. One of my stage guitarists would regularly 'bow out' of a song during a verse, turn off the volume on his instrument, and quickly tune in, jumping back in before the solo. Not only did it not bother me, it made me respect him more.

CHOOSING THE RIGHT STRINGS AND PICKS

Many varieties of guitar strings and picks exist. As you become more proficient, you may use a different gauge of strings or a thinner pick. Many of my expert guitarist friends use different strings and picks for each guitar style.

GUITAR PICKS - MATERIAL
• **Plastic (Celluloid, Nylon, Delrin):** Most common, offering a range of flexibility and thickness. Celluloid gives a warm tone, Nylon is durable and flexible, and Delrin is rigid and smooth.
• **Metal:** Provides a bright, sharp tone but can be harsh on strings and frets.
• **Wood:** Offers a unique, warm sound but can wear down quickly.
• **Tortex:** Similar to Delrin, providing a balanced tone with good durability.

GUITAR PICKS - THICKNESS

•**Thin (0.38mm - 0.73mm):** Good for strumming and light playing, offering a bright, crisp sound.
•**Medium (0.73mm - 0.88mm):** Versatile, suitable for strumming and picking, providing a balanced tone.
•**Heavy (0.88mm - 1.2mm):** Ideal for lead playing and precise picking, offering a fuller, more powerful sound.
•**Extra Heavy (1.2mm and above):** Offers maximum control and a deep, rich tone, suitable for heavy styles like metal.

GUITAR PICKS - SHAPE

•**Standard:** The most common teardrop shape.
•**Jazz:** Smaller with a sharper tip, ideal for precise playing.
•**Triangle:** Larger and more accessible to grip, suitable for beginners.
•**Sharkfin:** Versatile with multiple edges for different tones.

GUITAR STRINGS - MATERIAL

•**Steel:** Used in electric and acoustic guitars, offering a bright, crisp sound.
•**Nickel:** Common in electric guitar strings, providing a balanced tone with a smooth feel.
•**Phosphor Bronze:** Popular for acoustic guitars, offering a warm, rich tone with good durability.
•**Nylon:** Used in classical and flamenco guitars, providing a soft, mellow tone.

GUITAR STRINGS – GAUGE (Thickness):

•**Extra Light (0.010 - 0.047 inches):** Easier to play, ideal for beginners and fingerstyle playing, offering a bright tone.
•**Light (0.011 - 0.052 inches):** Good balance between ease of play and tone, suitable for various styles.
•**Medium (0.012 - 0.054 inches):** Offers a fuller sound with more volume and sustain but requires more finger strength.
•**Heavy (0.013 - 0.056 inches and above):** Provides the richest tone and highest volume, ideal for heavy strumming and tuning stability.

GUITAR STRINGS - COATING

•**Coated Strings:** Have a polymer coating to extend lifespan and reduce finger noise. They can feel smoother but slightly muted compared to uncoated strings.
•**Uncoated Strings:** Offer a traditional feel and tone but may not last as long as coated strings.

Platinum recording artist **Kenny Rogers** once said:

"The guitar is the easiest instrument to play, and the hardest to play well."

Tad Sisler and Family with Kenny Rogers
Source- Sisler Private Collection

GUITAR STRAPS
A comfortable, durable guitar strap goes a long way. The worst thing that can happen to a performer is when their strap fails in the middle of a performance, and the guitar falls and gets damaged. Make sure your strap is always securely attached to the guitar. Here are some considerations for guitar straps:

GUITAR STRAPS - MATERIAL
•**Leather:** Durable and offers a classic look. Leather straps can be plain or padded for extra comfort, making them suitable for extended playing sessions.
•**Nylon:** Affordable, lightweight, and available in various colors and designs. Nylon straps are great for beginners and casual players.
•**Polyester:** Like nylon, but often comes with printed designs. It provides a comfortable and secure fit.
•**Suede:** Offers a soft and luxurious feel with a good grip, preventing the strap from slipping off the shoulder.

GUITAR STRAPS - WIDTH
•**Narrow (2 inches or less):** Lightweight, easy to handle, and suitable for lighter guitars or short playing sessions.
•**Wide (2.5 to 4 inches):** Provides better weight distribution, reduces shoulder strain, and is ideal for heavier guitars or more extended playing periods.

GUITAR STRAPS - PADDING
•**Padded Straps:** Extra cushioning for added comfort, handy for extended playing times.
•**Non-Padded Straps:** Lightweight and uncomplicated, suitable for short-playing sessions or lightweight guitars.

GUITAR STRAPS - ADJUSTABILITY
•**Adjustable Length:** Allows players to customize the strap length for a comfortable playing position. Look for easy-to-adjust mechanisms like buckles or sliding adjusters.

GUITAR STRAPS - DESIGN
•**Plain:** Simple and functional, focusing on comfort and durability.
•**Decorative:** Featuring various patterns, embroidery, and designs to suit personal style and stage presence.

GUITAR STANDS
Stands can protect your guitar from damage, and you can put several guitars on stands for readiness on stage or in the studio. I've found that choosing stands can be motivated by your environment. For instance, a simple wall mount may work in a studio or at home. On stage, you'll want a durable stand that is hard to knock over when your burly bass player trips over it.

GUITAR STANDS - TYPES
•**A-Frame Stands:** Compact and portable, ideal for holding one guitar securely and folding for easy transport and storage.
•**Tubular Stands:** Feature a sturdy base with a neck cradle, providing more stability for heavier guitars. Some models are collapsible for portability.
•**Multi-Guitar Stands:** Designed to hold multiple guitars, making them perfect for studios or performances where quick access to different guitars is needed.
•**Wall Mounts:** Save floor space by mounting guitars on the wall. They provide a secure and decorative way to display guitars while keeping them easily accessible.
•**Hanging Stands:** Hold the guitar by the neck, often with padding to protect the finish. They offer good stability and are easy to use for quick guitar changes.

GUITAR STANDS - MATERIAL
•**Metal:** Provides durability and stability, suitable for home use and gigs.
•**Wood:** Offers a more aesthetic appeal and is often used for wall mounts and high-end stands.
•**Plastic:** Lightweight and portable, suitable for travel or casual use.

GUITAR STANDS - FEATURES
•**Padding:** Protects the guitar's finish from scratches and dents. Look for stands with foam or rubber padding.
•**Adjustability:** Some stands offer adjustable height and width to accommodate different guitar sizes and shapes.
•**Security:** Features like locking mechanisms or straps provide additional security, ensuring the guitar stays in place.

WHY HANG YOUR GUITAR ON THE WALL? More than likely, the safest place for your guitar is in a case unless the place where you store your guitar is subject to extreme fluctuations in temperature. Leaving your guitar in direct sunlight can warp the bridge. And in rare circumstances, extreme heat can also crack the soundboard.

The least safe place to store your guitar is on a floor stand. Anyone, including your dog or other musicians onstage (watch out for that burly bass player), can trip on the stand and send your guitar flying, cracking the headstock, or scratching your guitar. When you place your guitar on a padded hanger on the wall, it is safe, out of traffic, and easy to grab. And the downward pull of the guitar's weight takes some stress off the strings' pull in the other direction.

No matter how you store your guitar, it is vital to check the humidity in the room where your guitars are stored. Hygrometers are inexpensive, and you may want to use a humidifier, especially when you run your heat during the cold winter months. The main thing is to play and pamper your guitar as much as possible. The more attention it gets, the longer it should last!

Former **United States Secretary of State, General Colin Powell** said:

"There are no secrets to success. It's the result of preparation, hard work, and learning from failure."

Secretary of State, General Colin Powell and Tad Sisler
Source – Sisler Private Collection

GUITAR CAPOS: A guitar capo clamps onto the neck of a guitar, pressing down all the strings at a particular fret. By doing this, it effectively shortens the length of the strings, raising their pitch. The capo allows guitarists to change the key of a song without altering the chord shapes, making it easier to play in different keys. It can benefit vocalists who match their vocal range with the guitar's pitch.

One of the primary uses of a capo is to simplify chord progressions. For example, a song originally in the F Major key, which can be challenging for beginners due to barre chords, can be played using open chords by placing the capo on the first fret and playing the chord shapes of E major. Additionally, capos enable guitarists to explore different tonal possibilities and textures. By placing the capo in varying positions on the fretboard, players can achieve a variety of sounds and voicings that would otherwise require complex fingerings. This versatility makes the capo a valuable tool for studio recordings and live performances, allowing musicians to adapt songs quickly and efficiently.

GUITAR CASES AND PROTECTION: When I was younger, I was working more than a dozen gigs every week for extended periods, constantly moving my equipment. Because I didn't purchase cases for my keyboards or sleeves for my speakers, my equipment became extremely beat up, and I eventually became embarrassed to set it up. No matter how good you sound, people are also watching your appearance and presentation, and a good case is worth its cost in preventative protection over the long run.

GIG BAGS are lightweight, durable, soft cases made from nylon or polyester, offering protection from minor impact and scratches.
•**Pros:** Lightweight, portable, often with padded interiors and additional pockets for accessories.
•**Cons:** They provide less protection than hard cases, making them less suitable for air travel or heavy-duty use.

HARD CASES are sturdy, rigid cases typically made from wood, fiberglass, or moulded plastic. They offer excellent protection against impacts, moisture, and temperature changes.
•**Pros:** Provide superior protection for the guitar, ideal for touring musicians and air travel.
•**Cons:** Heavier and bulkier than gig bags, making them less convenient for casual use.

HYBRID CASES combine features of both gig bags and hard cases, offering a balance between protection and portability. They often have a semi-rigid frame with a padded interior.
•**Pros:** Lighter than hard cases but more protective than gig bags, suitable for frequent gigging.
•**Cons:** Typically, more expensive than gig bags and may still be less protective than fully hard cases.

FLIGHT CASES are heavy-duty cases designed for maximum protection during air travel and made from high-impact plastic or aluminum, including reinforced corners and heavy-duty latches.

•**Pros:** Flight cases offer the best protection against rough handling, temperature changes, and humidity.

•**Cons:** Very heavy and expensive, often used by professional musicians and touring bands.

Most of my friends do not check their guitars through with their luggage when flying to a gig. They almost always carry the guitar in a hard case or gig bag on the airplane.

SETTING UP YOUR PRACTICE SPACE: An excellent practice space allows you to go directly into a friendly environment and concentrate fully on the experience of learning and playing. Subtle considerations like using a comfortable chair without armrests are ideas you may not have already considered. It's surprising how wonderful it is to have your own space ready to go when you prepare to play!

SEATING: Use a chair with no armrests to avoid interference with arm movement. Ensure it provides adequate support for your back to maintain good posture. The chair should be at a height where your feet are flat on the ground and your thighs are parallel to the floor. Proper chair height helps maintain a natural and relaxed position.

GUITAR POSITION: The guitar should rest comfortably against your body. The neck should be angled slightly upwards to reduce strain on your fretting hand. Consider using a footstool under your left foot (if you're right-handed) to raise the leg and provide additional support, especially when playing classical guitar.

LIGHTING: Ensure the practice area is well-lit to avoid straining your eyes— position lighting to illuminate the guitar and music sheets without causing glare.

MUSIC STAND: Adjust a music stand to eye level to avoid bending your neck. The stand should be stable and easily adjustable.

ACCESSORIES AND ORGANIZATION: Keep all accessories like picks, tuners, capos, and music sheets within easy reach to avoid unnecessary movement and maintain focus.

TEMPERATURE AND HUMIDITY CONTROL: Maintain a consistent temperature and humidity level to protect your guitar from damage and to ensure a comfortable practice environment.

BREAKS AND STRETCHING: Take regular breaks to avoid repetitive strain injuries. Stretch your fingers, wrists, and arms to keep them flexible and reduce tension.

CABLE MANAGEMENT: Neatly organize cables to prevent tripping hazards using electric equipment.

IMPORTANCE OF A QUIET, DEDICATED SPACE
A quiet, dedicated space minimizes distractions and allows for focused practice sessions. This environment helps improve concentration and facilitates the development of muscle memory, enables consistent setup and organization of equipment, making it easier to maintain a productive practice routine.

"Let the music breathe." – David Gilmour

David Gilmour
Credit – Wikimedia Commons

ORGANIZING YOUR MATERIALS
When all necessary items, such as sheet music, picks, tuners, and capos, are easily accessible and systematically arranged, it minimizes interruptions and allows for more focused practice sessions. This organization helps quickly transition between exercises and techniques, fostering a more seamless learning experience.

LIGHTING AND AMBIANCE
Make sure to have good lighting to clearly see your sheet music, fretboard, and other materials, reducing eye strain and improving posture. A well-lit space helps maintain focus and prevents mistakes caused by poor visibility. I painted my studio a specific color of green because I read that the government did a study of colors that enhance creativity and steady workflow, and this particular green scored high! Ambiance is more critical than you may realize.

CREATING A PRACTICE SCHEDULE: Finding time for anything is impossible in today's world, so you need to make time. Regular practice helps build muscle memory, improves technique, and keeps motivation high. Setting specific times for practice allows you to create a routine that integrates guitar playing into your daily life, making it less likely to be skipped. Additionally, a structured schedule can help track progress and set short-term and long-term goals, making learning more efficient and rewarding. To start, consider practicing for 20-30 minutes daily. Increase the duration as your skill improves and you build stamina. Additionally, diversify your practice sessions by alternating between different techniques, like scales, chord progressions, and songs, to consistently maintain interest and challenge yourself.

CHAPTER THREE
GETTING ACQUAINTED WITH YOUR INSTRUMENT

K nowing everything about how your guitar works makes you realize it is similar to an organism. Everything works in symmetry because of the intricate way the guitar is put together. When all the parts work and a guitar is tuned correctly, it is truly a work of art.

UNDERSTANDING GUITAR ANATOMY

Your guitar consists of a **Headstock, Neck** and **Body**.

HEADSTOCK

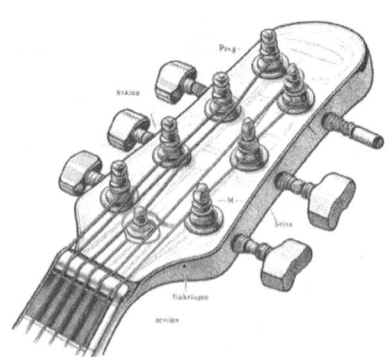

The **Headstock** contains the tuning pegs, allowing you to adjust the strings' tension and effectively tune the guitar. The strings are inserted into the tuning pegs, wound, and settled into the **Nut**, a metal bar between the Headstock and the neck of the guitar.

The **Nut** is sometimes made of bone or plastic. It has shallow grooves, guiding the strings and maintaining their height and spacing. The **Nut** is crucial in determining the action and intonation of your guitar.

NECK

The **Neck** of the guitar contains the frets (metal strips embedded on the **Fretboard**) and fret wire, allowing the player to change the tone of each string by placing their finger between the frets.

The **Fretboard**, sometimes called the **Fingerboard**, is a meticulously crafted, thin, flat surface attached to the front of the Neck. It's usually made of hardwood like maple or rosewood. The **Fretboard** has metal **Frets** embedded into it. When you press the strings against the frets, you naturally change the pitch of the notes.

Frets are the metal strips embedded into the **Fretboard** at specific intervals, dividing the **Neck** into semitones, allowing you to press the strings against them, creating different notes and chords.

BODY

The **Body** of the guitar contains the sound hole (on acoustic and acoustic/electric guitars), allowing the guitar to produce a louder, fuller, and richer sound. The table or top plate of the **Body** holds the **Saddle.**

The **Bridge,** a powerful conductor of musical energy, is located on the front of the **Body**. It anchors the strings, acting as a **base** and **Saddle**, holding them securely in place. More than that, it's a **key** player in the symphony of sound, transferring the vibrations from the strings into the **Body**, creating the guitar's overall sound.

The **Saddle**, a versatile plate on the far end of the table, is where the strings originate on the guitar. It's not just a part of the guitar, it's your partner in perfecting your playing. It allows you to adjust the action, or the distance between the fret board and the strings, enabling you to play the guitar more effortlessly, enhancing your musical journey.

In the **Saddle**, you place metal **pick-ups** on electric guitars, picking up the strings' sound and amplifying the guitar from an outside source. Different **pick-ups** produce different qualities of sound.

Pick-ups consist of magnets wrapped with copper wire coils, picking up the vibrations and converting them into electric signals, sending signals to an **amp** or **speaker**.

Some electric guitars also contain a **whammy bar**, a metal bar placed on the Body allowing the guitarist to 'bend' the strings by using the bar, creating a unique effect.

"Playing guitar is like telling the truth. You can bend it, distort it, dress it up, and make it sparkle, but the truth will always come out in the end."
— Prince

Prince
Credit: Wikimedia Commons

Electric guitars also feature **Control Knobs**, allowing you to adjust various parameters, including volume and tone, affecting the output level and tonal characteristics of your guitar.

The **Output Jack** connects the guitar to an amp or other audio equipment, transferring the electric signals from the pickups to external devices through a cord or wireless system.

STRAP BUTTONS are at the base of the **Neck** and the bottom of the body, providing attachment points for your **Guitar Strap**, should you choose to use one. **Straps** work best when performing while standing or performing on stage.

The **Truss Rod** is a metal rod embedded within the **Neck**, enabling you to adjust the **Neck's** curvature or neck relief. When you alter the tension on the **Truss Rod**, you can correct any issues you find relating to string action and the bowing of the **Neck**, usually caused by changes in temperature and humidity.

Inlays are those fantastic decorative elements embedded into the fretboard, sometimes made of mother-of-pearl, taking the form of blocks, dots, or intricate designs. **Inlays** are aesthetically beautiful and functional as they provide visual reference points for the player.

KNOWING YOUR INSTRUMENT

Understanding how a guitar works allows you to appreciate the guitar's construction better, which may help you make better choices when selecting new guitars. It's all about exploring the endless possibilities for your creative expression.

Iconic singer **Glen Campbell** had a string of #1 hits, but few people knew just how great a guitar player he was. He told a story of how he had to improvise his setup when he was young:

"I needed a capo – a clamp to hold down the strings – so my daddy made me one out of a corn on the cob and a rubber band."

Glen Campbell performing with Tad Sisler
Source- Sisler Private Collection

LEFT-HANDED GUITAR PLAYING: Paul McCartney is probably the most famous left-handed guitar player of all time. The guitar was designed for a right-handed person. This is not to say that not many left-handed virtuosos play the guitar exactly as it is, exceptionally well! But a left-handed person just beginning to learn to play does have options.

One practical option is to purchase a 'left-handed' guitar, which essentially flips the guitar around, enabling you to play it as a right-handed person would. This allows you to use your dominant hand for picking or strumming and your other hand for chording, making the learning process more intuitive.

You can also achieve the same primary result by just restringing your guitar in reverse order and flipping it over. Just remember that most lessons are planned around a right-hand guitar, so it may be difficult to find learning materials to play left-handed.

"My guitar is like my best friend. My guitar can get me through anything. If I can sit down and write an amazing song with my guitar about what's going on in life, then that's the greatest therapy for me."
— Miley Cyrus

Miley Cyrus
Credit – Wikimedia Commons

TUNING YOUR GUITAR

I've already delved into tuning methods and the importance of always having a tuned guitar.

When tuning, remember the basics: Guitar tuning methods vary based on the desired pitch and tone for different styles of music. The most common method is standard tuning of each string (EADGBE) to a specific pitch. But what about exploring beyond the norm? Alternate tunings, such as drop D (DADGBE), lower the sixth string for a deeper sound, often used in rock and metal. Open tunings, like open G (DGDGBD), tune the strings to form a chord when played open, popular in slide guitar and blues. DADGAD tuning is favoured in Celtic music for its drone-like sound. And then, there are custom tunings, a realm of endless possibilities. These are tailored to individual playing styles and compositions, allowing guitarists to create their own unique sonic landscapes. So, why not embark on your own tuning journey?

ELECTRONIC VS. EAR TUNING

"I learned to tune a guitar by ear. That method has served me pretty well." – Charley Pride

Electronic guitar tuning, using devices like tuners or tuning apps, offers precision, speed, and convenience, especially in noisy environments where it's hard to hear the strings. It ensures accuracy by providing exact pitch readings, which is helpful for beginners and professionals. However, relying solely on electronic tuners can inhibit the development of a musician's ear training and ability to discern pitch. Ear tuning, on the other hand, enhances a musician's listening skills and deepens their understanding of musical intervals and harmonies. While it can be time-consuming and challenging, particularly for beginners or in loud settings, ear tuning fosters a more intuitive connection with the instrument and music overall.

Begin by tuning the low E string (6th string) to a piano, tuning fork, or another in-tune instrument. Once the low E string is correctly tuned, press down on the [5th fret of the E string] to produce an A note, and adjust the open A string (5th string) until it matches this pitch. This process is then repeated for the remaining strings: press the [5th fret - A string] to tune the open D string (4th string), the [5th fret - D string] to tune the open G string (3rd string), the [4th fret - G string] to tune the open B string (2nd string), and finally the [5th fret - B string] to tune the open high E string (1st string). Make minor adjustments while listening carefully until all strings are in tune with each other.

TROUBLESHOOTING COMMON TUNING ISSUES

Start by ensuring the strings are properly stretched and not overly worn, as old strings can cause tuning instability. Inspect the tuning pegs for looseness; tighten them to maintain string tension. Check the nut and bridge for obstructions or rough spots that impede string movement and cause uneven tension. Ensure the guitar neck is appropriately adjusted, as neck bowing can affect intonation and tuning stability. Additionally, examine the guitar for any loose hardware or structural issues. Regular maintenance, such as cleaning the fretboard and lubricating the nut, can also help keep the guitar in tune.

MAINTAINING TUNING STABILITY:

By regularly maintaining your guitar, you can significantly enhance its tuning stability. Regularly changing strings and properly stretching them after installation helps prevent slippage. Ensure the tuning pegs are tight and functional and consider using locking tuners for added stability. Lubricate the nut and bridge to reduce friction that can cause tuning drift, especially when using the tremolo or bending strings. Keep the guitar in a stable environment with consistent temperature and humidity, as fluctuations sometimes expand or contract the wood, affecting tuning. Regular neck adjustments and intonation checks ensure the guitar remains properly set up.

"Gonna wind it up on my guitar. Gonna make that silver sing."
— Tom Petty in "Dreamville"

Tom Petty
Credit- Wikipedia Commons

CHAPTER FOUR
BASIC GUITAR CARE

We've already touched on the importance of many aspects of caring for your guitar. Here are the fundamentals of basic guitar care:

CLEANING YOUR GUITAR

Begin by wiping down the strings with a soft, dry cloth. This process removes oils and sweat, which can cause corrosion. For deeper cleaning, loosen or remove the strings to access the fretboard and body more efficiently. Use a guitar-specific cleaner or a damp cloth to gently clean the fretboard, removing dirt and grime that can accumulate over time. For unfinished fretboards like rosewood or ebony, consider applying a small amount of lemon oil to condition the wood, but avoid using it on finished maple fretboards.

You can clean the guitar's body with a guitar polish and a microfiber cloth, which helps remove dust, smudges, and fingerprints without scratching the finish. Pay attention to areas around the pickups, bridge, and other hardware, using a small, soft brush to reach tight spots. Regularly check and clean the tuning pegs and other metal parts to prevent rust.

CHANGING STRINGS

Regularly changing strings will help to prevent a string from breaking while you're performing. Changing strings on a guitar is a straightforward process that can significantly enhance the instrument's playability and tone. Start by loosening the old strings using the tuning pegs until they are slack enough to remove. Carefully unwind each string from the tuning peg and remove it from the bridge. For guitars with bridge pins, gently pull out the pins to release the strings. Clean the fretboard and other areas usually covered by the strings before installing the new strings.

INSTALLING NEW STRINGS

1. Carefully string the ball end of each string into the bridge and replace the bridge pins if applicable, ensuring they are secure.
2. Guide the other end of the string through the corresponding tuning peg hole, leaving some slack.
3. Begin winding the string by turning the tuning peg, making sure the string wraps neatly around the peg and tightens smoothly.
4. Repeat this for each string, tuning them roughly to pitch as you go.
5. Once all strings are in place, stretch them gently to help them settle, and then tune the guitar accurately.
6. Trim any excess string length from the tuning pegs, and you can play with your newly restrung guitar.

STORING YOUR GUITAR SAFELY

Remember the advice we've already given you to store your guitar safely on the wall or in a case in a controlled environment.

HANDLING TEMPERATURE AND HUMIDITY CHANGES

Remember our advice about keeping your guitar in a controlled environment. Guitars, especially those made of wood, are sensitive. Even slight fluctuations in humidity or temperature can expand, contract, or crack the wood. To manage this, keep the guitar in a room with consistent conditions, ideally between 65-75°F (18-24°C) and 45-55% relative humidity. When traveling with your guitar, allow it to acclimate gradually to new environments by keeping it in its case and avoiding sudden temperature changes.

REGULAR MAINTENANCE TIPS

String Care: Regularly wipe down your strings after playing to remove oils and sweat, which can cause corrosion. Change strings every few months or sooner to maintain optimal tone and playability.

Cleaning: Keep your guitar clean by wiping down the body, neck, and hardware with a soft, dry cloth after each use. Periodically use guitar-specific cleaners and polishes to remove dirt and fingerprints and condition the fretboard with lemon oil (for unfinished wood) to prevent drying and cracking.

Humidity and Temperature Control: Store your guitar in a safe, stable environment, ensuring consistent temperature and humidity levels. Use a hygrometer to monitor conditions and employ a humidifier or dehumidifier to protect the wood from warping or cracking.

Neck and Fretboard Maintenance: Regularly check the neck for proper relief and adjust the truss rod if necessary. Clean the fretboard to remove grime and polish the frets to keep them smooth and free of oxidation.

Hardware Checks: Inspect and tighten any loose hardware, including tuning pegs, strap buttons, and screws. Ensure the bridge and nut are in good condition and adjust or replace to maintain proper intonation and playability.

CHAPTER FIVE
SETTING YOUR GOALS

IMPORTANCE OF REALISTIC GOALS

B efore we get into the basics of setting short-term and long-term goals, let's start with the most important goal you can set, which is to practice as much as you can. Your attitudes and emotions are second; they will carry you through any challenge if aligned with your goals.

PRACTICE MAKES PERFECT

Develop a **practice routine**—set **goals** on how to hone your skills more efficiently.

"There is an old saying: The harder you try the luckier you get. I kind of like that definition of luck." – President Gerald R. Ford

Tad with President Gerald Ford
Source – Sisler Private Collection

There's a saying that if you do something repeatedly for 21 days, it becomes a habit. In the same manner, practicing regularly, at least for 30 minutes each day, will benefit you in so many ways. Not only will you become exponentially better at your craft, but you will also feel more **relaxed** and **confident** physiologically.

Many musicians, including myself, have experienced the gripping fear of **stage fright**. When I first started performing, I would sit outside the nightclub for a few minutes before I went in, praying for the strength to face all of these people and hoping they would like me. The nature of being an artist is that you never know how people will accept you, so we are often insecure. Remember, you are not alone in this struggle.

Fortunately, the **better** you play, the more **confident** you'll be. If you have natural stage fright, Practice in front of a mirror or play in front of trusted family members or friends, gradually working your way into performing in front of strangers. The more you play, the more relaxed you become, allowing you to deliver captivating performances.

The great actress **Mary Tyler Moore** said:

"Take chances, make mistakes. That's how you grow. Pain nourishes your courage. You have to fail in order to practice being brave."

Tad Sisler with Mary Tyler Moore
Source- Sisler Private Collection

The term **"Woodshedding"** has unknown origins. However, I read somewhere that the great trumpeter **Doc Severinsen** coined the phrase when, in his early years, he went into the woodshed behind his house to practice his trumpet for hours on end. So, shred while you shed!

"Personally, I think young musicians need to learn to play more than one style. Jazz can only enhance the classical side, and classical can only enhance the jazz. I started out playing classical, because you have to have that as a foundation." – Doc Severinsen

Doc Severinsen
Credit: Wikimedia Commons

IT'S ALL ABOUT YOUR MINDSET

Passion and **persistence** are the building blocks of the mindset of the guitar virtuoso. Really, **persistence** is everything.

"Nothing in this world can take the place of persistence. Talent will not; nothing is more common than unsuccessful men with talent."
– President Calvin Coolidge

Nothing great comes without a struggle. The idea is to embrace the journey and do everything possible to stay motivated through all the challenges ahead.

VISUALIZE YOUR SUCCESS – In my early days, I would often find solace in prayer, seeking guidance and confidence before I stepped into my first gigs. It was all about visualizing my success. Fear, I realized, was just an impostor. A dear friend **of mine, Frank Hamblen**, a 7-Time Championship-Winning NBA Coach with **Michael Jordan's** *Bulls* and **Kobe Bryant's** *Lakers*, said:

"You just refuse to lose. True success is found in the relentless pursuit of excellence and the unwavering belief in your own potential."

Frank Hamblen and Tad Sisler
Source – Sisler Private Collection

So many people quit right when success is literally around the corner. Tell yourself, **"Failure is not an option."**

Musicality will get you there. The more you deeply understand music, the more you'll learn to express yourself authentically.
The best way to get there is to collaborate and network, build connections with fellow musicians, and constantly explore new growth opportunities.

Very importantly, do everything you can to give the appearance of being successful, and the best way to do that is to experience the joy and fulfillment you get when you perform, and others will notice!

You will gain insights and new techniques by following this **roadmap** to your guitar mastery. Remember, it's a journey that doesn't end until we stop breathing; if you're good at it, you never want it to end.

Every small step you take matters. My good friend, Hall of Fame *Major League Baseball* pitcher **Trevor Hoffman** said:

"Confidence is everything. If you start second guessing yourself, you're bound to run into more bad outings."

Tad Sisler with Trevor Hoffman
Source – Sisler Private Collection

ACHIEVABLE SHORT-TERM GOALS

President Bill Clinton was known to be able to easily encapsulate issues. The President worked with each problem singularly until he had a solution that he felt worked, and then he moved on to the next problem. When you're overwhelmed with too much information around you in today's world, the most excellent skill you can develop is how to encapsulate tasks into individual chunks rather than trying to take on everything at once. Learning how to encapsulate and achieve small milestones is the value of setting short-term goals. Here are a handful of examples of achievable short-term goals when learning to play guitar:

Learn Basic Chords: Memorize and smoothly transition between common open chords such as G, C, D, E, A, and F.

Strumming Patterns: Master a few basic strumming patterns for different songs.

Play a Simple Song: Learn to play a simple song from start to finish using basic chords and strumming.

Finger Exercises: Practice finger exercises daily to improve finger strength and dexterity.

Tuning by Ear: Develop the ability to tune your guitar by ear using reference pitches.

Learn a Scale: Memorize and play the major or minor pentatonic scale.

Barre Chord Practice: Start practicing barre chords to build finger strength and familiarity with more complex chord shapes.

Basic Music Theory: Music Theory is essential, even simply learning the notes on the fretboard and constructing major and minor chords.

TRACKING PROGRESS

Tracking progress in learning guitar involves outlining goals as we've done above. Breaking goals into smaller, more manageable tasks and creating a practice schedule to ensure consistent progress will propel you forward.

Maintain a practice journal to record daily or weekly activities, noting which exercises you've completed, the duration of practice sessions, and any difficulties encountered. This journal can also reflect on what went well and what needs improvement.

"If you want music to be your livelihood, then play, play, play and play! And eventually, you'll get to where you want to be." — Eddie Van Halen

Additionally, periodically record yourself playing to assess your progress over time objectively. Listening to these recordings allows you to identify areas needing work and celebrate improvements. Keep your motivation high.

"Nothing is more rewarding than to take a song, create it out of thin air and then watch it affect people." — Luke Bryan

Luke Bryan
Credit – Wikimedia Commons

REWARDING YOURSELF

As you achieve your goal of becoming a better guitarist, rewarding yourself can help maintain motivation and make the learning process enjoyable. Here are a few ways to reward progress:

New Equipment: Treat yourself to a new guitar accessory, such as a capo, a set of high-quality strings, a guitar strap, or even a new pedal or tuner. Small rewards keep you excited about practicing while enhancing your playing experience.

Music and Lessons: Purchase sheet music or a songbook for your favorite songs. Alternatively, reward yourself with a professional lesson or workshop to further hone your skills and learn new techniques.

Recording Gear: Invest in essential recording equipment, such as a USB microphone or an audio interface, to start recording your playing. Purchasing and using recording equipment serves as a reward and helps you track progress and share your music.

Concerts and Events: Attend a live concert of your favorite artist or band. Experiencing live music can be incredibly inspiring and reinforce your passion for learning guitar.

Personal Milestones: Celebrate achievements with a small treat or experience, like a special meal, a day out, or a relaxing activity you enjoy.

Keep yourself motivated and excited about achieving new guitar-playing milestones!

Sister Rosetta Tharpe was called the *"Godmother of Rock and Roll."* She was a pioneer who blended gospel music with electric guitar. She influenced a generation of musicians with her innovative style and powerful voice, including **Elvis Presley** and **Chuck Berry.** She set many short and long-term goals in a competitive and racially challenged environment and attained them through persistence. Study her work to round out your rock performances.

Sister Rosetta Tharpe
Credit: SynCallio on DeviantArt/Wikimediacommons.org

ADJUSTING GOALS AS YOU IMPROVE

Initially, goals might focus on basic skills such as learning open chords, simple strumming patterns, and playing easy songs. Once you master basic chords, a new short-term goal could be to learn and incorporate barre chords, which require more finger strength and precision.

Additionally, as technical abilities improve, goals should include more complex techniques and musical styles, like learning fingerpicking patterns, exploring different genres, or mastering soloing and improvisation using scales and arpeggios. Continually set and adjust goals beyond your current capabilities.

SETTING ATTAINABLE LONG-TERM GOALS

Here are a handful of ambitious yet attainable long-term goals for learning how to become a great guitarist:

Master Multiple Genres: Develop proficiency in playing musical styles like rock, blues, jazz, classical, and fingerstyle to become a versatile guitarist.

Improvisation Skills: Achieve fluency in improvisation, creating solos and riffs spontaneously in any key or genre.

Advanced Techniques: Master advanced guitar techniques such as sweep picking, tapping, hybrid picking, and complex chord voicings.

Music Theory Knowledge: Gain a deep understanding of music theory, including scales, modes, chord progressions, and harmony, and apply this knowledge to your playing and composition.

Original Composition: Write, record, and produce your original music, showcasing your skills and creativity as a guitarist.

Professional Performance: Perform regularly in live settings, solo or with a band, to build stage presence and confidence.

Teaching and Mentoring: Develop the ability to teach guitar, sharing your knowledge and skills with others through private lessons, workshops, or online tutorials.

Session Work and Collaboration: Become proficient in studio recording and as a session guitarist, collaborating with other musicians and contributing to diverse musical projects.

CREATING A TIMELINE

As with anything worthwhile, looking at the big picture of what's ahead is an excellent idea. For me, learning to play my instrument was hammered into me from age five, so it became a part of who I am at a very early age. It was in my blood to learn and love the process, which certainly makes it much easier to excel. Make it a burning desire, and you will be bound to succeed. No matter how old you are when you start, you can achieve anything you want with persistence and patience. Look about five years ahead to a realistic timeline to becoming a master of the guitar:

TIMELINE FOR LONG-TERM SUCCESS

Months 1-3: Foundation Building

Goal: Establish basic skills and familiarity with the instrument.

• Learn and memorize basic open chords (G, C, D, E, A, F).
• Practice simple strumming patterns and switching between chords.
• Learn to tune the guitar by ear and with an electronic tuner.
• Play a few simple songs from start to finish.
• Develop a consistent practice routine (15-30 minutes daily).

Months 4-6: Intermediate Skills Development

Goal: Enhance playing techniques and build confidence.

• Introduce barre chords and practice smooth transitions.
• Learn basic scales (e.g., major, minor pentatonic) and practice them daily.
• Start basic fingerpicking patterns.
• Play along with backing tracks to develop timing and rhythm.
• Begin to explore music theory basics (notes on the fretboard, intervals).

Months 7-12: Expanding Techniques and Repertoire

Goal: Broaden your playing style and technical abilities.

• Master more complex strumming patterns and fingerpicking techniques.
• Learn and practice more advanced scales and modes (e.g., blues scale, Dorian mode).
• Work on developing improvisation skills within different keys.
• Learn songs from various genres to diversify your repertoire.
• Start recording yourself to track progress and identify areas for improvement.

Year 2: Advanced Techniques and Musicality

Goal: Achieve technical proficiency and deeper musical understanding.

• Master advanced techniques such as hammer-ons, pull-offs, slides, bends, and vibrato.
• Dive deeper into music theory, learning chord construction, and more complex progressions.
• Begin writing and composing music.
• Gain experience playing with other musicians. Join a band.
• Perform live at open mics or small venues to build stage presence.

Year 3: Mastery and Professional Development

Goal: Refine skills to a professional level and explore diverse musical opportunities.

• Perfect advanced guitar techniques include sweep picking, tapping, and hybrid picking.
• Continue to write, record, and produce original music.
• Develop a teaching plan and start offering beginner guitar lessons.

- Work on becoming proficient in multiple genres (jazz, classical, rock, blues).
- Seek opportunities for session work, collaborations, and studio recording.

Beyond Year 3: Continuous Improvement and Innovation

Goal: Sustain growth, innovate, and contribute to the musical community.
- Regularly set new goals and challenges to keep progressing.
- Innovate by experimenting with new styles, techniques, and technology.
- Share your knowledge through workshops, online content, or publications.
- Continue performing, recording, and collaborating with other musicians.
- Maintain a passion for learning and a dedication to continuous improvement.

This timeline provides a structured but flexible approach to mastering guitar over the long term, allowing for personal adjustments and growth at your own pace. Remember, everything worth doing looks daunting when you first start, but remember the words of **Lao Tzu**, *"The journey of a thousand miles begins with a single step."*

Orianthi is an Australian guitarist who performed with **Michael Jackson, Alice Cooper**, and **Carlos Santana**. Study her solos, and her ability to seamlessly blend pop, rock, and blues. She is truly a virtuoso who developed a similar timeline and achieved her goals regularly until she made it all the way.

Orianthi
Credit – RSO, Richie Sambora, Orianthi – CreativeCommons.org

RESOURCES TO HELP YOU REACH YOUR GOALS

Whether you learn from a book, a private instructor, or an app, there are a thousand great resources to help you become a great guitarist. Experience is the best teacher, so get out there and play as much as possible!

I've compiled a list of resources available to help a guitarist achieve long-term goals, along with their sources. I neither endorse nor am I affiliated with any of these sources, and we strongly suggest that you research anything carefully before spending money on it! However, many musician friends have greatly benefited from these and others. **Gibson** has a great app too for learning guitar.

ONLINE GUITAR LESSONS AND COURSES

Fender Play: Offers step-by-step lessons for beginners to advanced players. https://www.fender.com/play

Justin Guitar: Free lessons from Justin Sandercoe, covering various styles and techniques. **https://www.justinguitar.com/**

TrueFire: Extensive library of video lessons and courses from renowned guitar instructors. **https://truefire.com/online-guitar-lessons**

YOUTUBE CHANNELS

Marty Music: Tutorials and lessons on songs, techniques, and theory. https://www.youtube.com/user/martyzsong

JamPlay: Learn from Grammy Award Winners. https://www.youtube.com/user/jamplaydotcom

BOOKS AND METHOD GUIDES

"Hal Leonard Guitar Method": Comprehensive method books for learning guitar. **https://www.halleonard.com/**

"The Guitar Handbook" by Ralph Denyer: Detailed guide covering everything from basics to advanced techniques. https://www.scribd.com/document/435421339/the-Guitar-Handbook

PRACTICE TOOLS AND APPLICATIONS

Yousician: Interactive app providing feedback on your playing and structured lessons. **https://yousician.com/?bx=true**

Guitar Pro: Software for writing, learning, and practicing guitar tablature. **https://www.guitar-pro.com/**

See our section on AI-Powered apps for more suggestions.

FORUMS AND COMMUNITIES

Ultimate Guitar: Online community with forums, tabs, and lessons. **https://www.ultimate-guitar.com/**

Reddit - r/Guitar: This is an active subreddit where guitarists share tips, ask questions, and discuss gear. **https://www.reddit.com/r/Guitar/?rdt=43288**

JAM TRACKS AND BACKING TRACKS

JamPlay: Offers a variety of jam tracks for practice and improvisation. **https://jamplay.com/**

Quist: Provides a variety of high-quality backing tracks in different genres and keys, perfect for practicing improvisation and soloing. **https://www.youtube.com/user/QuistTV**

PROFESSIONAL INSTRUCTION

In-person or online lessons with a qualified instructor can provide personalized guidance. **Yamaha** has quite a few tremendous private lesson programs. We've also heard great things about **Lessonface.**: **https://www.lessonface.com/**

Attend workshops or masterclasses by renowned guitarists to learn advanced techniques. Music festivals, guitar conventions, or websites like **https://www.masterclass.com/**

I love the **MasterClass** website, which is an excellent resource for learning anything from the Masters.

MUSIC COLLEGES/UNITED STATES:

Schools like the **Musicians Institute** in Hollywood, CA are completely acceptable. **MI** has an excellent vocal, drum, guitar, and audio engineering program. I have friends who work with headliner artists and compose for film and television who have graduated from **MI**. Here are some more prestigious schools of music education:

Juilliard School (New York, NY): **Juilliard** is renowned for its rigorous training and high standards, offering voice and opera performance degrees. Its alumni include **Renee Fleming, Nina Simone, Audra McDonald**, and **David Bryan.**

Berklee College of Music (Boston, MA): Known for its contemporary music programs, **Berklee offers** extensive vocal performance programs, including jazz and popular music. It has a diverse curriculum and notable alumni like **John Mayer** and **Esperanza Spalding**. This program has a high bar for qualification, so you should be excellent and prepared to be the best.

Curtis Institute of Music (Philadelphia, PA): **Curtis** is highly selective, admitting only a few students each year, and provides full-tuition scholarships to all its students. It focuses on classical and opera training with a strong emphasis on performance.

Indiana University Jacobs School of Music (Bloomington, IN): One of the largest music schools in the **United States, Jacobs** offers various programs and degrees in vocal performance. It has a notable faculty and alumni network, including **Joshua Bell** and **Leonard Slatkin.**

New England Conservatory of Music (Boston, MA): **NEC** offers comprehensive programs in voice and opera, with a strong emphasis on performance and musicianship. It is deeply integrated into **Boston's** vibrant music scene.

MUSIC COLLEGES/EUROPE:

Royal College of Music (London, UK): Founded in 1882, this institution is consistently ranked as one of the top music schools globally, offering a wide range of degrees in various musical disciplines and boasting top-notch facilities and a distinguished faculty.

Royal Conservatoire of Scotland (Glasgow, Scotland): Known for its excellent music, drama, and dance programs, the **Royal Conservatoire of Scotland** hosts over 500 public performances each year, providing ample performance opportunities for students.

Royal Academy of Music (London, UK): The oldest conservatoire in the UK, founded in 1822, the **Royal Academy of Music** offers a range of programs from Bachelor's Degrees to advanced diplomas. It has a rich history of producing celebrated musicians such as **Elton John** and **Annie Lennox.**

Conservatoire National Supérieur de Musique et de Danse de Paris (CNSMDP) (Paris, France): Established in 1795, **CNSMDP** is one of **Europe's** leading institutions for music and dance, with comprehensive programs in musical disciplines.

Universität für Musik und darstellende Kunst Wien (Vienna, Austria): Located in **Vienna**, a city renowned for its classical music heritage, this university offers many music degrees. It is one of the largest and most prestigious music schools in **Europe.**

These resources can help guitarists set and achieve long-term goals, from improving technical skills to broadening their musical knowledge and performance abilities.

"You can only make a good noise on the guitar if you're committed. Little careful noise doesn't work. You have to be bold."
— Hans Zimmer

Hans Zimmer
Credit: Creative Commons

STAYING MOTIVATED

Staying motivated over the long haul while learning to become a better guitarist involves setting realistic goals, maintaining variety in practice, seeking inspiration, and connecting with a supportive community. Here are some strategies:

Set Realistic Goals: Break down long-term goals into smaller, manageable milestones. Celebrate each achievement to maintain a sense of progress and accomplishment.

Variety in Practice: Incorporate a mix of exercises, songs, and techniques in your practice routine to keep things interesting. Alternate between scales, chord progressions, fingerpicking, and strumming patterns to prevent monotony.

Seek Inspiration: Regularly listen to various music and watch performances by your favorite guitarists. Discovering new styles and techniques can reignite your passion and provide new goals to strive for.

Record and Reflect: Record your playing to track your progress. Reviewing past recordings can highlight your improvements and motivate you to continue practicing.

Join a Community: Engage with other guitarists through local music groups, online forums, or social media. Sharing challenges, experiences, and successes with others can provide encouragement and new perspectives.

Learn New Songs: Continuously add new songs to your repertoire. Learning songs you love can make practice enjoyable and give you a tangible sense of achievement.

Take Breaks: Avoid burnout by taking short breaks when needed. Step away from the guitar to rest and return with renewed energy and focus.

Attend Live Performances: Going to concerts and live performances can be incredibly motivating. Seeing skilled musicians perform can inspire you to practice and improve your playing.

Take Lessons: Periodically take lessons from a skilled instructor. A teacher can provide new challenges, personalized feedback, and align your practice routine with your goals.

Reward Yourself: Set a reward system for achieving certain milestones. Treat yourself to new gear, a special outing, or something you enjoy celebrating your progress.

Remember, **experience** is the greatest teacher. I did a solo for seven years when I first started performing professionally. I got better, but I got exponentially better when I surrounded myself with great musicians and learned from them as I gained experience through my storied career.

What did the experience teach me? I learned way more than any theory and harmony course could teach me. However, I used my knowledge of the fundamentals of music along with my early classical training to create the foundation of what I became.

Music is math. Theory and harmony provide the foundation for a greater understanding of music, just as Geometry does to architecture and Calculus to computer programming. The knowledge you gain provides a benchmark for critical thinking. You use it in more ways than you would ever imagine without knowing it!

Start by building your **foundation** and remember that the potential for greatness lies within your fingertips, waiting to be discovered. Be persistent in your practice and unlock the master musician within you. Strive to become an extraordinary guitar player, and in the process, you might just discover a new side of yourself.

Playing in a group is like engaging in a team sport. It's not just playing your part; it's about connecting with others and learning from the experience. My dear friend, legendary **NFL** lineman **Junior Seau** said:

"I didn't play the game for the money or the fame. I played because I loved the game. It was my sanctuary, my escape, and my way of connecting with something greater than myself. Football taught me discipline, resilience, and the importance of teamwork. It shaped me into the person I am today, and for that, I will forever be grateful."

Tad Sisler with NFL Hall of Famer Junior Seau
Source – Sisler Private Collection

You could easily substitute "playing in a band" for "football," and you wouldn't be far off. Band gigs are a team sport. I've performed with many musicians on stage, and there's nothing better than syncing with another great musician or group, knowing you're killing it.

EVALUATING AND REVISING YOUR GOALS

As you progress to become a better guitarist, assess your strengths and areas that need improvement by recording your playing, seeking feedback from teachers or peers, and comparing your progress against your initial objectives. Set aside time every few months to review your practice routine and adjust it to incorporate new emerging techniques, genres, or musical interests.

Don't be afraid to set your sights higher as you conquer your short-term goals. For instance, if you've mastered basic chords and strumming patterns, challenge yourself to learn advanced techniques like fingerstyle, soloing, or improvisation. Introduce new goals that foster creativity, such as writing original music or performing live. Be open to adjusting your goals as your interests and opportunities evolve, like joining a band or participating in workshops.

PHYSICAL AND MEDICAL BENEFITS

My father, **Maynard Lee Sisler,** was a physician specializing in internal medicine. He learned medicine on the spot as a medic on a Navy ship in World War II. Doctors were scarce in the South Pacific, so my father quickly learned to diagnose sailors and do emergency surgery when needed. Years later, after extensive training in medical school, he told me that the most important thing a doctor can do is to listen to their patients. In their own way, they will tell you what you need to know to help them. I believe it's the same with all of us. We must learn to listen to ourselves and what our body and mind tell us. Most of what is wrong with us can be helped immensely by exercise, eating right, and getting enough sleep.

Maynard Lee Sisler, M.D., F.A.C.P.
Source – Sisler Private collection

When things get rough, I remind myself how blessed and fortunate I am to have the outlet of playing an instrument. Playing an instrument offers numerous medical benefits, significantly contributing to physical health and well-being. Regular practice enhances fine motor skills, requiring precise finger movements and hand-eye coordination. People recovering from injuries or those with conditions like arthritis can benefit greatly from playing an instrument, as it can help improve dexterity and strength.

> *"If I don't practice one day, I know it; two days, the critics know it; three days, the public knows it." - Jascha Heifetz*

Additionally, playing an instrument can have cardiovascular benefits, as it often involves rhythmic breathing and sustained physical activity, which can improve lung capacity and heart health. It also promotes better posture and can alleviate physical tension, reducing the risk of musculoskeletal issues.

Psychologically, playing an instrument can profoundly impact mental health and cognitive function. It has been shown to reduce stress, anxiety, and depression by providing an emotional outlet and fostering a sense of accomplishment and self-expression. Music practice stimulates brain regions involved in memory, attention, and spatial-temporal skills, potentially enhancing cognitive abilities and delaying cognitive decline in older adults. Studies confirm that regularly playing an instrument can slow or even prevent the onset of Alzheimer's and Parkinson's diseases in some patients.

> *"For me, the guitar is the most expressive instrument there is. It can mirror your every mood, from sweet and gentle to fierce and powerful." – Jimmy Page*

On a strictly psychological level, **Jimmy Page** highlights the guitar's ability to reflect the players emotions and dynamic range, encouraging you to connect deeply with your instrument.

My sister, **Suzanne Ramsey**, was a trained psychologist and a mental health center director for many years. She told me that she found in many patients that simple stress and burnout were the cause of many mental health issues. Fears, including fear of failure or disappointment, were other leading issues beyond simple depression based upon loss. Learning to sing or play an instrument can help to alleviate many mental health issues, and a recent study in *Science Daily* showed that playing an instrument and learning music have been linked to better brain health in older adults. My sister had many tools to help her patients, and music therapy was among those tools.

Suzanne Ramsey and Tad Sisler
Source- Sisler Private Collection

Playing an instrument also promotes discipline, patience, and perseverance, which can improve overall mental resilience. Additionally, it encourages social interaction and a sense of community through group play and performances, contributing to improved mood and emotional well-being.

So, in addition to becoming a guitar hero and blessing others with your talent, you are also doing wonders for yourself medically, spiritually and psychologically!

"When the intellectual part of guitar playing overrides the spiritual, you don't get to extreme heights." – John Frusciante

John Frusciante
Credit – Simple English Wikipedia

CHAPTER SIX
FINDING INSPIRATION

I've filled this book with inspirational quotes and ideas. Staying inspired is the key to becoming great at whatever you do. There is a joy and powerful feeling when you play 'air guitar' while listening to your favorite guitar solo. Multiply that by ten when you learn how to play that solo yourself. But never forget the feeling you felt with the imaginary guitar in your hands.

"A child playing air guitar plays no wrong notes." – Victor Wooten

FAMOUS GUITARISTS AND THEIR JOURNEYS: Here are a few inspirational stories of famous guitarists and their journeys:

I.   **Jimi Hendrix:** Hendrix's journey is overcoming adversity and pushing musical boundaries. Growing up in poverty, he taught himself to play guitar by ear. Despite initial setbacks and struggles to succeed, his innovative approach to the electric guitar, blending blues, rock, and psychedelia, eventually made him a legend, inspiring countless musicians with his creativity and technical prowess. His iconic song **"Purple Haze"** is associated with the psychedelic rock movement. Its iconic opening riff and innovative guitar effects showcase Hendrix's revolutionary approach to the instrument.

> *"Don't use your brain to play it, let your feelings guide your fingers."*
> *— Jimi Hendrix*

Jimi Hendrix emphasized the importance of playing with instinct and emotion instead of overthinking. This approach leads to more expressive music.

2.   **Carlos Santana: Santana's** unique fusion of Latin rhythms with rock and blues has made him a pioneering figure in music. He marked his journey from Mexico to global stardom with his relentless dedication and spiritual approach to music. His breakthrough performance at *Woodstock* and subsequent success showcased his passion and innovation, inspiring generations of musicians and leading to his biggest hit, **"Smooth,"** with **Rob Thomas** in 1999. His rendition of **"Europa"** remains one of the most sensual, passionate ballads ever played on the guitar.

> *"The guitar is a vehicle for expressing your heart and soul. It's a way to communicate the deepest parts of yourself without saying a word."*
> *— Carlos Santana*

Carlos Santana emphasizes the guitar as a tool for your own personal expression, encouraging you to focus on conveying emotion through your music.

3.   **Stevie Ray Vaughan**: Overcoming drug addiction and a near-fatal helicopter crash, **Vaughan's** journey is one of redemption and extraordinary talent. His passionate and powerful blues guitar playing revitalized the genre in the 1980s. **Vaughan's** determination, resilience, and virtuosic skill left a legacy after his untimely death. His biggest hit, **"Pride and Joy,"** is a high-energy blues-rock track showcasing Vaughan's exceptional guitar skills, soulful vocals, and signature Texas blues sound.

> *"I fell in love with the guitar because it's like having a best friend that never lets you down." — Stevie Ray Vaughan*

Stevie Ray Vaughan had a personal and emotional connection with the guitar, which helped him to keep pushing through challenges.

4.   **B.B. King**: Starting as a street musician in Mississippi, **King's** rise to fame was driven by his relentless work ethic and emotional connection to the blues.

His signature style earned him the title **King of the Blues. King's** journey from humble beginnings to global recognition is a testament to his dedication and influence. I opened for **B.B. King** when I was a younger man. I remember hearing him credit **Frank Sinatra** for helping him break the color barrier in music. His biggest hit, **"The Thrill Is Gone,"** is a soulful blues classic characterized by passionate vocals, poignant lyrics about lost love, and **King's** expressive guitar playing, featuring his distinctive vibrato and melodic phrasing.

5.   **Joan Jett**: Facing gender barriers in the rock industry, **Jett** broke boundaries and found persistence. As the frontwoman of **The Runaways** and later with the **Blackhearts**, she fought for her place in a male-dominated field. Her anthem, **"I Love Rock 'n' Roll,"** and her unwavering attitude have inspired many women to pursue music careers.

6.   **Django Reinhardt**: Despite losing the use of two fingers on his left hand in a fire, **Reinhardt** became one of the most influential jazz guitarists of all time. His innovative playing style and the creation of gypsy jazz demonstrated his resilience and creativity. **Reinhardt's** story is an inspiring example of overcoming physical limitations to achieve greatness.

Django Reinhardt
Credit- Wikipedia Commons

7.   **Eddie Van Halen**: Known for his groundbreaking techniques like tapping, **Van Halen** revolutionized rock guitar playing. His journey from a young immigrant in the United States to a rock icon is filled with innovation and musical exploration. **Van Halen's** technical mastery and energetic performances have inspired countless guitarists. One of my friends was present at **Van Halen's** first audition in front of record label executives. He performed with his back to the group so that nobody could witness (and perhaps steal) his signature tapping technique, where he used both hands on the guitar neck to produce rapid and complex note sequences. He got the record deal!

"When I play guitar, it's the closest thing to flying. The instrument becomes an extension of myself, and there's nothing else like it."
— Eddie Van Halen

Eddie Van Halen regularly compared playing guitar to a transcendent experience, believing that the instrument becomes a part of the player.

8. **Bonnie Raitt**: A slide guitar virtuoso and blues singer, **Raitt's** career spans decades of musical excellence. She faced industry resistance and personal struggles but remained dedicated to her craft. Her breakthrough with the album **"Nick of Time"** and continued success highlight her resilience and commitment to authenticity in music.

I could go on and on with countless stories of people like you and me who overcame unique challenges to become greats. Still, I know many great guitarists who never achieved fame in the manner that everyone knows their name. Yet, they still made outstanding contributions to their genre. Others, like **Terry Kath,** are generally overlooked in the dustbin of history. However, few people know that when **Jimi Hendrix** saw **Kath** play with the legendary group **"Chicago"**, he commented that **Terry** was the greatest guitarist he had ever seen.

You may have never heard of **Tommy Tedesco, Danny Kortchmar,** or **Waddy Wachtel,** but these guitarists had more of a profound influence on modern popular style and technique than most of the greats combined. Study their work. So, remember, it doesn't have to be about fame or fortune, each coming with joys and challenges. If you contribute to your art form and move people with your performances, these elements will make you a success.

EXPLORING DIFFERENT GENRES: Just as different performers choose different guitars to emulate their style, specific genres lend themselves to types of guitars, choice of strings, methods of playing, and many other elements.

This book wouldn't be complete without the mention of **Nancy Wilson**, a founding member of the rock band **Heart.** She had the fantastic ability to blend rock, folk, and classical influences into her playing, which defined **Heart's** sound and kept this group relevant for over four decades.

Nancy Wilson
Credit – Wikimedia Commons

Blending genres is an outstanding characteristic in a rounded guitarist. My friend **Chad Quist** is in a **Heart** tribute band, and he can duplicate these intricate guitar parts as if they were his own, along with a thousand other changes and licks he plays perfectly. Plus, **Chad** has an excellent singing voice. While you're studying **Nancy Wilson's** guitar sounds and music, check out **Chad Quist's** originals. You'll be glad you did.

Chad Quist
Source – Chad Quist

A guitarist can play a wide range of genres, each with its unique characteristics and techniques. The most popular are:

1. **Rock**: Characterized by solid and driving rhythms, power chords, and electric guitar solos, rock encompasses various subgenres like classic rock, punk rock, and hard rock.

2. **Blues**: Known for its expressive bends, vibrato, and the 12-bar blues structure, blues guitar playing often involves soulful improvisation and emotional intensity.

3. **Jazz**: Jazz guitar features complex chord voicings, improvisation, and syncopated rhythms, often blending elements of swing, bebop, and fusion styles.

4. **Classical**: Classical guitar focuses on fingerstyle techniques, intricate compositions, and using nylon-string guitars to play pieces from composers like Bach, Sor, and Tarrega.

5. **Country**: Country guitar playing includes techniques like fingerpicking, chicken picking, and twangy, bright tones, often featuring storytelling through the music.

6. **Metal**: Metal guitar is characterized by heavy distortion, fast riffs, palm muting, and techniques like shredding and tapping, often creating aggressive and assertive sounds.

7. **Folk**: Folk guitar emphasizes acoustic playing, fingerpicking patterns, and simple, melodic strumming, often supporting lyrical storytelling and traditional tunes.

8.   **Reggae**: Reggae guitar features offbeat rhythms, known as skanking, with a focus on rhythm guitar to create the genre's characteristic laid-back, syncopated feel.

9.   **Flamenco**: Flamenco guitar involves rapid fingerpicking, percussive techniques, and intricate melodies, often performed on nylon-string guitars, reflecting its Spanish roots.

10. **Funk**: Funk guitar is known for its rhythmic, percussive playing style, using techniques like muting and syncopated strumming to create tight, danceable grooves.

11. **Pop**: Pop guitar playing is versatile, often incorporating elements from various genres to create catchy, accessible melodies and rhythms suitable for mainstream appeal.

12. **Latin**: Latin guitar encompasses styles like bossa nova, samba, and salsa, using syncopated rhythms, fingerstyle techniques, and rich harmonic progressions.

In today's world, when you choose a genre you want to explore, the greatest gift you can give yourself is to find the top five most influential guitarists within that genre and listen, studying their finger techniques, how they develop their particular sounds, and their unique approaches. You'll be surprised as you improve in that genre how you borrow from everyone you hear, sometimes without even realizing it. Soon, you will generate your unique style of performance.

My great friends, **Michael Higgins**, and **Brian Nova** are stellar guitarists; both studied under the legend **Joe Pass**. **Brian Nova** put together an outstanding teaching course that I highly recommend. **Michael Higgins** and I have recorded about a thousand songs in multiple genres, including jazz, rock, country music, baroque, renaissance, and classical. **Michael's** solo classical guitar albums perfectly exemplify acoustic guitar mastery with nylon strings. His contemporary jazz albums rank among the best in the business. Check out both **Brian Nova's** and **Michael Higgin's** music for inspiration and tutelage.

Tad Sisler with Michael Higgins
Source – Sisler Private Collection

KEEPING A PRACTICE JOURNAL

A practice journal for a guitarist is a dedicated notebook or digital document where the musician meticulously tracks their practice sessions, goals, and progress. Each entry typically includes the date, duration of the practice, specific exercises or pieces worked on, and any observations or challenges encountered.

You can monitor your development and identify areas for improvement by logging details such as scales, chord progressions, songs, or techniques practiced. This structured approach helps maintain a consistent practice routine and ensures that you systematically address all aspects of guitar playing.

In addition to daily logs, set weekly or monthly goals and review your achievements and setbacks at the end of each period. The journal can also be a repository for notes on music theory, inspirational quotes, or feedback from lessons and performances.

Fundamental techniques such as proper finger placement, strumming, fingerpicking, and fundamental chord transitions form the backbone of guitar playing, ensuring precision, speed, and fluidity. These basics also promote good habits and prevent injuries, laying the groundwork for complex techniques like soloing, improvisation, and intricate fingerstyle patterns.

CHAPTER SEVEN
ESSENTIAL PERFORMANCE TECHNIQUES

"Every time you pick up your guitar to play, play as if it's the last time." -
Eric Clapton

MASTERING STRUMMING AND PICKING

Strumming is sweeping your pick or fingers across the strings, producing chords or rhythmic patterns. Begin your strumming journey by mastering the basic **downstrokes. This fundamental technique involves** strumming downwards on the beat, while counting 1,2,3,4. It's crucial to maintain a steady rhythm, as this will serve as the foundation for your strumming skills.

Move to alternating **downstrokes and upstrokes**, creating a flow of continuous strumming, down-up-down-up.

Once you've mastered the art of strumming, it's time to add some flair. Try **syncopating** your downstrokes and upstrokes or adding accents to specific strums. This technique, often called 'making it breathe,' can add depth and emotion to your playing. Still, few of us can make it 'gently weep' like **George Harrison** did, filling each performance with emotion.

Picking involves using a guitar pick (or a plectrum) or using your fingers to pluck individual strings, producing melodies, intricate patterns, or even arpeggios.

Alternate your downstrokes and upstrokes as you pick, playing single notes each time. Alternating will help you improve your speed and precision.

"Speed is a by-product of accuracy." — Guthrie Govan

As a harpist might play, **fingerpicking accomplishes** the same feat with your finger instead of picking, plucking the strings individually, or using fingerstyle patterns. As you improve, minimize your excess movement by picking in the direction of the next string you will play, using downstrokes and upstrokes to accomplish this style of **economy picking**.

Once you've honed your strumming and picking skills, it's time to take it up a notch. By combining your pick and finger techniques, you can expand your repertoire and play more complex arrangements. This versatile approach will not only enhance your playing but also open a world of musical possibilities.

The **Righteous Brothers** had the #1 played song on American radio in the 20th century with their platinum #1 *Billboard* chart hit, **"You've Lost That Lovin' Feelin'."** **Righteous Brothers** founder and lead singer **Bill Medley** said:

"Passion: It's what separates a singer from an entertainer. I hope I have passion for my music, my family, and my friends until they start shovelling dirt on my face."

Tad Sisler with the Righteous Brothers
Source – Sisler Private Collection

Start slowly, gradually increasing **speed** as you concentrate on **accuracy** and build **muscle memory** in your playing. **Practice,** and then **practice** some more.

"Learn the basics, and then forget them." - Jimi Hendrix

It can be true! I had to 'unlearn' much of the formal training I got when I went out into the world and performed in a thousand different environments. Learn everything you can, embrace it, and make it a part of who you are as you move forward.

CIRCLE OF FIFTHS

Take the time to learn music theory and harmony to become a more rounded player. Start with the circle of fifths. Learning this helps you with theory, key signatures, chord progressions, and scale patterns:

Key Signatures: The circle of fifths visually shows you the relationship between different key signatures, making identifying sharps and flats in any key easier, helping you adapt quickly to different songs and genres.

Chord Progressions: Many common chord progressions in music follow the circle of fifths, such as I-IV-V or ii-V-I, helping you to anticipate chord changes and create more effective bass lines.

Improvisation: The circle of fifths helps you understand which chords and scales work well together, making it easier to improvise and create melodic bass lines that fit harmonically within a song.

Transposing: Knowing the circle of fifths helps you to transpose songs into different keys when you perform with other musicians or adapt to vocal ranges.

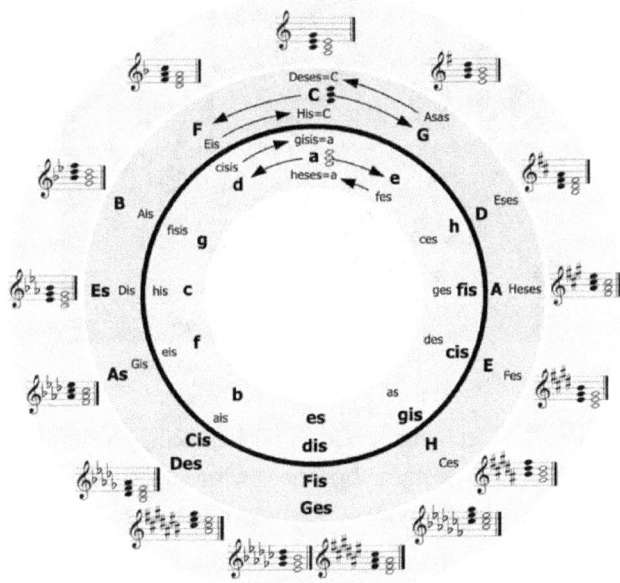

Circle of Fifths

Credit – Wikimedia Commons

Use a **metronome** to work on your **timing**. A common joke is... *"so many drummers, so little time."* You can learn as much technique as you want, but if you don't develop your timing along the way, you will find yourself a seriously flawed player.

Although I prefer a professional live drummer anytime, I've perfected my **timing** using drum machines, which act as sophisticated metronomes without you even knowing it. After a while, it becomes a part of your playing when you get away from the metronome, and you know instantly when you start to rush, or someone else starts to rush. So many otherwise talented drummers have driven me crazy, slowly playing a little faster as the song drags on. On the other hand, there's nothing more exhilarating than playing with a band where your drummer and bass player are right in the pocket all night.

Stress the significance of maintaining a **relaxed, comfortable position** while playing. This not only minimizes fatigue and tension but also enhances your overall performance.

"The best advice I've ever got is to be yourself. Stay true to who you are and what you stand for and you'll go far in life." – Snoop Dogg

Snoop Dogg and Tad Sisler
Source – Sisler Private Collection

Never stop learning! Watch **tutorials** or take **lessons** to build your arsenal of strumming patterns and picking techniques. One of my secrets early on was to surround myself with players who were better than me, which lifted me and made me better.

Immerse yourself in the **power of inspiration.** By analyzing the playing styles of guitarists across genres, you can fuel your own creative development. Each style has its unique charm, and by appreciating and learning from them, you can add a touch of their magic to your own playing.

"A good player can make any guitar sound good." Michael Bloomfield

>>

Before we continue, I have a small favor to ask of you…

MAKE A DIFFERENCE WITH YOUR BOOK REVIEW
Unlock the Power of Kindness
"When we share our music, we help others find joy."

I've been lucky to work with many amazing guitar players over the years. I've seen music production grow from big tape machines and huge outboard effects racks to advanced computers with recording software and plug-ins. Through it all, I learned that knowing your instrument in depth enough to give emotional performances can help you to move and influence others with your unique talent. That's why I wrote this book—to help you know, love, and master guitar from top to bottom.

Would you help someone just like you—curious about playing guitar but unsure where to start?

My mission is to make playing guitar easy, fun, rewarding, and successful for everyone.

But to reach more people, I need your help.

Most people choose books based on reviews. So, I'm asking you to help another guitarist by leaving a review.

It doesn't cost anything and takes less than a minute, but it could change someone's musical journey. Your review could help...

- ...one more person learn to play guitar.
- ...one more child discover the joy of music.
- ...one more student gain confidence.
- ...one more dream come true.

If you purchased my book on Amazon, here's the link to leave your review:

https://www.amazon.com/review/review-your-purchases/?asin=1966258011

Or, you can just use this QR code to access the review page on Amazon:

If you love helping others, you're my kind of person, and... your honest review will mean the world to me. Thank you from the bottom of my heart!
Tad Sisler

IMPORTANCE OF PROPER POSTURE
Good players can make any guitar sound good because of all the elements they've learned about being well-rounded. One of the most essential elements is posture.

Proper posture significantly impacts performance and long-term physical health, and helps prevent strain and injuries, particularly to the back, neck, and shoulders, which are common among guitarists due to prolonged practice sessions. It allows for better hand positioning and movement, facilitating smoother transitions and more precise playing. Good posture enhances breathing and promotes overall endurance and comfort. By prioritizing ergonomic positioning from the start, you can ensure more effective practice sessions and longevity in your playing career.

When I was young, my mother ran her finger down my back and said, *"Put your angel wings back."* This exercise was her reminder for me to have good posture.

STEP-BY-STEP GUIDE TO PROPER POSTURE

If you took our advice earlier in the book and set up a proper practice space, you're on track to integrate good posture into your routine.

Choose the Right Chair: Use a chair without armrests and with a straight back to support your spine. Ensure your feet are flat on the ground and your thighs are parallel to the floor.

Sit Upright: Sit up straight. Do not slouch or lean forward or backward. Support your back with the chair.

Position Your Legs: Keep your legs at a natural angle. Playing an acoustic or classical guitar, you might use a footstool to elevate your left leg slightly.

Hold the Guitar Properly: Right-handed players rest the guitar on the right thigh. Angle the neck slightly upward, with the guitar's body close to your body.

Left Hand Position: Your left thumb should rest lightly on the back of the guitar neck. Your fingers should curve naturally over the fretboard without pressing too hard.

Right Hand Position: Rest your right forearm on the upper part of the guitar body. Your wrist should be relaxed, and your fingers should be free to move across the strings without tension.

Maintain a Relaxed Posture: Relax your shoulders. Do not hunch your shoulders. Keep your head aligned with your spine, avoiding forward or backward tilting.

Adjust As Needed: Make minor adjustments to your position regularly to avoid stiffness. If you experience any discomfort, reassess your posture and make necessary changes.

COMMON POSTURE MISTAKES TO AVOID

When developing good posture, avoid several common mistakes. First, avoid slouching or hunching over the guitar, leading to back and neck strain over time. Ensure your shoulders remain relaxed and not raised or tense. Refrain from placing the guitar too low or too high on your body; it should sit comfortably on your thigh with the neck at a slight upward angle. Avoid gripping the guitar's neck too tightly with your left hand, which can cause unnecessary tension and hinder finger mobility. Also, make sure your right wrist is balanced when picking or strumming. Finally, avoid sitting for long periods without breaks, as prolonged practice without movement can lead to stiffness and discomfort.

> *"Lean your body forward slightly to support the guitar against your chest, for the poetry of music should resound in your heart."*
> *– Andrés Segovia*

EXERCISES TO IMPROVE POSTURE

Seated Forward Bends: Sit on the floor with legs extended. Bend forward from the hips, reaching for your toes. This stretches the lower back and hamstrings, promoting flexibility and a straighter spine.

Shoulder Rolls: Sit or stand with your back straight. Slowly roll your shoulders forward in a circular motion for 10 reps, then reverse and roll them backward. This helps to release tension in the shoulders and upper back.

Wall Angels: Stand with your back against a wall, feet slightly away from it. Press your lower back, upper back, and head against the wall. Raise your arms to shoulder height and bend your elbows so your hands point upward. Slowly move your arms up and down, keeping contact with the wall. This exercise helps strengthen the upper back and improve shoulder alignment.

Cat-Cow Stretch: Get on all fours with your hands under your shoulders and knees under your hips. Alternate between arching your back (cat pose) and dipping it (cow pose).
This movement increases spinal flexibility and promotes a neutral spine posture.

Thoracic Extension: Sit on a chair with a backrest at shoulder height. Place your hands behind your head and gently lean back over the chair, extending your upper back. This exercise helps counteract the forward hunch from playing guitar.

Neck Stretches: Sit or stand with your back straight. Slowly tilt your head towards one shoulder, holding the stretch for 20-30 seconds. Repeat on the other side. This helps alleviate tension in the neck muscles.

Seated Spinal Twist: Sit on a chair or the floor with legs extended. Cross one leg over the other and place the opposite hand on the outside of the crossed knee. Twist your torso towards the crossed leg, using your hand for leverage. This exercise improves spinal flexibility and alignment.

HAND POSITIONS

We just mentioned the benefits of proper hand positions for improving your posture, and we described proper hand positioning in the steps above.

Here are a handful of exercises for guitarists to strengthen their hand positions:

Finger Stretches: Gently stretch each finger by pulling it back towards your wrist with your other hand. Hold for 10-15 seconds on each finger. This exercise improves flexibility and reduces tension.

Spider Exercise: Place your fingers on the fretboard, one finger per fret. Play each note sequentially. Start on the first fret with your index finger (index, middle, ring, pinky) on one string, then move to the next. This exercise enhances finger independence and strength.

Chromatic Scale Exercise: Play a chromatic scale up and down the fretboard using all four fingers, moving one fret at a time. This exercise builds dexterity and coordination.

Finger Lifts: Place your fingers on the fretboard in a starting position. Lift one finger at a time, then place it back down. Repeat with each finger to improve control and strength.

Hammer-Ons and Pull-Offs: Practice hammer-ons and pull-offs between each pair of fingers on one string. This exercise helps to build finger strength and agility.

Finger Rolls: Place your index finger on the first fret and roll it to play the adjacent string without lifting the finger. Repeat with each finger. This exercise improves finger flexibility and control.

Stretch and Reach: Place your fingers on widely spaced frets (e.g., index on 1st fret, middle on 3rd fret, ring on 5th fret, pinky on 7th fret). Hold and release, then shift positions. This exercise enhances reach and flexibility.

Finger Push-Ups: Place your hand flat on a table, lift one finger at a time, and lower it back down. Repeat for each finger to build strength.

"I just plug in and let go." — Billy Joe Armstrong

Billy Joe Armstrong
Credit- Wikimedia Commons

AVOIDING HAND STRAIN AND INJURY

While you're concentrating on all of these methods, we're giving you to become a great guitarist, it's easy to get caught up in the mechanics of what you're doing and forget that, at some point, all of this will be second nature to you, and you'll plug in and let go.

I have a friend who is a brilliant classical guitarist. He teaches at local colleges and does about 300 gigs per year. He played so much in one year that his elbow became inflamed like a 'tennis elbow.' He worked through it, but it was painful and uncomfortable. Even the best players can't always avoid injury.

However, a guitarist can avoid hand strain and injury by adopting several preventive measures. First, ensure proper posture and hand positioning to minimize unnecessary tension and promote natural alignment. Regularly incorporate hand and finger stretching exercises before and after playing to maintain flexibility and reduce stiffness.

Take frequent breaks during long practice sessions. Let your muscles rest and recover. Gradually increase practice intensity and duration to build endurance without overexerting the hands. Ergonomic accessories, such as adequately adjusted guitar straps and supportive seating, can also help prevent strain.

Lastly, paying attention to any discomfort and addressing it promptly with rest or professional advice is crucial to avoiding more severe injuries.

HAND POSITIONING TECHNIQUES

Keep working it until it feels comfortable, using these techniques and others you'll pick up yourself with experience:

Proper Thumb Placement: Position the thumb on the back of the guitar neck, roughly opposite the middle finger, providing a stable pivot point. This exercise helps maintain finger strength and skill.

Curved Fingers: Keep your fingers naturally curved when pressing down on the strings. This positioning allows for more precise and clean fretting.

Finger Perpendicularity: Ensure your fingers press the strings perpendicularly to avoid muting adjacent strings and to produce clear notes.

Light Pressure: Apply only the necessary pressure to the strings to avoid strain. Excessive force can lead to fatigue and injury over time.

Wrist Alignment: Maintain a straight or slightly bent wrist to reduce tension and prevent conditions like carpal tunnel syndrome. Avoid extreme bends that can cause strain.

Hand Relaxation: Keep your hand relaxed, avoiding unnecessary tension. Regularly check for and release any tightness during practice.

Use All Fingers: Utilize all four fingers (index, middle, ring, and pinky) to improve overall agility and reach across the fretboard.

Alternate Picking: For the picking hand, use alternate picking (downstroke followed by upstroke) to increase speed and efficiency while reducing strain.

BASIC STRUMMING TECHNIQUES

Section One described strumming using downstrokes, upstrokes, syncopation, picking, fingerpicking, alternating downstrokes and upstrokes, and economy picking.

"I believe every guitar player inherently has something unique about their playing. They just have to identify what makes them different and develop it." – Jimmy Page

Before any guitarist develops a style, they must "woodshed" the fundamentals of strumming and picking while learning their chord structures and other performance nuances. Here are exercises a guitarist can do to improve various strumming and picking techniques:

STRUMMING EXERCISES

Basic Downstrokes: Practice strumming down on each beat of a 4/4 time signature. A metronome or click track will help maintain a steady rhythm. Gradually increase the tempo as you become more comfortable.

Upstrokes: Practice upstrokes by strumming upwards on the "and" of each beat, using a 4/4 time signature. Combine with downstrokes to create a steady down-up pattern.

Alternating Downstrokes and Upstrokes: Strum down on the beat and up on the "and" to create a consistent down-up pattern. Practice with a metronome, starting slow and gradually increasing speed.

Syncopation: Strum in patterns that emphasize off-beats or weak beats. For example, strum down on 1, up on the "and" of 2, down on 3, and up on the "and" of 4. This action creates a syncopated rhythm.

PICKING EXERCISES

Alternate Picking: Practice picking a scale or simple melody using alternate picking (down-up-down-up). Start slow and focus on evenness between downstrokes and upstrokes.

Economy Picking: Practice scales using economy picking, which involves using a single pick stroke for consecutive notes on adjacent strings. For example, if moving from a downstroke on the 3rd string to a note on the 2nd string, use a downstroke for the following note.

FINGERPICKING EXERCISES

Basic Fingerpicking Pattern: Practice the basic fingerpicking pattern: P (thumb) on the 6th string, I (index) on the 3rd string, M (middle) on the 2nd string, A (ring) on the 1st string. Create a simple arpeggio pattern and practice it slowly.

Travis Picking is named after country and western guitarist **Merle Travis.** He popularized this fingerpicking style in the 1940s and 1950s, using his thumb to play alternating bass notes on the lower strings. In comparison, his index finger plucked melody notes on the higher strings, creating a syncopated rhythm that became his signature style. This style is handy for solo C&W players, combining rhythm and melody with a bass note and picking style backing up their vocals. Check out the songs *"Sixteen Tons"* and *"Cannonball Rag"* to study this style.

Practice **Travis Picking** by alternating the thumb between the bass notes (6th and 4th strings or 5th and 4th strings) while the index and middle fingers pick out a melody on the higher strings. We'll delve more into fingerpicking in our chapter about advanced playing.

To further appreciate fingerstyle playing, study the work of Tommy Emmanuel. An Australian fingerstyle guitarist, Emmanuel's journey is marked by his dedication to mastering the instrument. As a child prodigy, he developed a unique solo acoustic style blending various genres. His story is one of continuous learning and passion for the guitar, earning him recognition as one of the greatest acoustic guitarists. His instrumental version of **"Classical Gas"** showcases his virtuosic technique, intricate melodies, and dynamic playing, blending classical, folk, and pop influences into a captivating performance.

Tommy Emmanuel
Credit – Wikipedia Commons

SYNCOPATION EXERCISES

Create strumming patterns that accentuate off-beats. For example, strum down on 1, up on the "and" of 2, skip 3, strum up on the "and" of 3, down on 4, and up on the "and" of 4. Practice with a metronome.

COMBINING TECHNIQUES

Combine all techniques into complex strumming and picking patterns. For example, you can integrate alternating picking with syncopated strumming. You can combine Travis picking with syncopated rhythms to develop versatility and improve overall technique.

Susan Tedeschi is known as a masterful blues guitarist and singer, with a powerful voice and soulful use of strumming and sophisticated rhythms in blues and roots music. **Susan** won a *Grammy Award* with the **Tedeschi Trucks Band**, and guitarists would do well to emulate her style.

Susan Tedeschi
Credit – Wikimedia Commons

STRUMMING WITH A PICK VS. FINGERS

Most guitarists I know will choose between using a pick or just using their fingers based upon the song, genre, guitar they are playing, or vibe they are trying to create, rather than choosing one over the other generally. Here are some pros and cons of using a pick vs. your fingers when playing:

STRUMMING WITH A PICK

PROS: Using a pick generally produces a louder and brighter sound, making it suitable for styles where projection is essential, such as rock and metal. A pick allows for faster and more precise strumming and picking, which is beneficial for playing intricate solos, speedy riffs, and complex strumming patterns. Picks provide a consistent tone and attack, ensuring uniformity in the sound produced across different strings and chords. With a pick, guitarists can efficiently execute techniques such as tremolo picking, alternate picking, and sweep picking.

CONS: Picks can limit the guitarist's ability to control dynamics and subtle nuances compared to fingerstyle playing. As a beginner, you may find holding and manoeuvring your pick challenging, leading to dropped picks and inconsistent playing initially. Some styles, particularly those requiring intricate fingerpicking patterns or softer tones, are more challenging to execute with a pick.

STRUMMING WITH FINGERS

PROS: Fingerstyle playing allows for greater control over dynamics and expressiveness, enabling subtle variations in tone and volume. Fingerstyle techniques are essential for genres like classical, flamenco, and folk, where intricate fingerpicking patterns are common. Using fingers can provide a more natural connection to the instrument, allowing for new tones and textures depending on how you pluck the strings. Fingerstyle playing enables the guitarist to play multiple independent lines simultaneously, such as bass lines, melodies, and chords.

CONS: Fingers typically produce a softer and warmer sound than picks, which may be better for genres requiring high volume and brightness. Achieving the same level of speed and precision as with a pick can be more challenging, particularly for fast solos and complex riffs. Prolonged fingerstyle playing can lead to finger fatigue and strain, primarily if proper technique is not maintained. Many guitarists grow and maintain their nails for optimal fingerstyle tone, which can require additional care and attention.

Both methods offer unique advantages and challenges, and many guitarists choose to master both to maximize their versatility and adaptability across different musical styles.

INCORPORATING DYNAMICS IN STRUMMING

As a **Yamaha Corporation of America** developer for over ten years, I learned a lot about programming guitar parts for keyboards. Our superiors taught us many ways of taking the sound of each string and maximizing the dynamics to make the sound soulful and realistic.

Dynamics are variations in softness and loudness, which add emotional depth and texture to a performance. By varying the intensity of strumming, a guitarist can highlight different song sections, emphasize beats, and convey the intended mood. For instance, softer strumming can create a sense of intimacy and delicacy, suitable for verses or quieter passages. In comparison, louder strumming can build intensity and excitement for choruses or climactic moments. This contrast helps to maintain the listener's interest and provides a more compelling musical experience. It allows for better balance and blending with different instruments, contributing to a cohesive and well-rounded performance. For example, in a band, the guitarist can adjust their strumming dynamics to complement the vocalist or to stay in sync with the drummer's accents. This sensitivity to dynamics improves the overall sound and demonstrates the guitarist's musicality and adaptability.

Legendary guitarist **Bill Frisell** was a master of dynamics. He demonstrated his outstanding ability during his rendition of *"Over the Rainbow,"* where he gradually increased his attack using emotional intensity throughout the performance. He explained that dynamics are about articulation over volume. **Frisell** accomplished this by varying his touch from soft, whispering notes to sharp, percussive accents, creating a story with his guitar and guiding the listener through an emotional journey. Remember, volume is only one way of intensifying a performance. Intensifying your performance through articulative peaks and valleys will solidify solid and emotional moments.

Bill Frisell
Credit- Wikimedia Commons

CHAPTER EIGHT
PLAYING CHORDS

UNDERSTANDING CHORD PROGRESSIONS

Combining multiple notes and playing them simultaneously produces **chords.** This combination is the harmonic foundation for a song. We generally characterize **chords** as major, minor, augmented, or diminished, with many variations.

OPEN CHORDS

If you are a beginner, start by learning the basic open **chords** in major keys. Open chords on the guitar are a fundamental aspect of playing and are often the first chords beginners learn. We call these chords "open" because they incorporate open strings, which are strings played without pressing down on any frets. Open chords typically use three or more strings and are played in the first three guitar frets.

BASIC OPEN CHORD SHAPES

The most common open chords include C major, G major, D major, E major, A major, and their minor counterparts (Am, Dm, Em). Each of these chords has a unique shape and finger positioning, which helps beginners develop finger strength and dexterity. Practicing these chords enables guitarists to quickly switch between chords, important for rhythm guitar playing. Open chords are used extensively in various genres, including folk, rock, pop, and country music, due to their rich, full sound and ease of play.

Work on your **transition** between chords, moving accurately and smoothly, starting with simple progressions and working to progress in complexity.

The more you know about the **theory** behind chord progressions, the more you'll understand how different **combinations** of chords work better together, leading you to create your progressions. Practice strumming with open chords, starting with simple songs, and you'll continue growing exponentially.

The easiest way to achieve this is to start with songs you like, identify the chords and progressions in the song, and assist you in recognizing common patterns. Listening and learning are excellent **ear training**.

SONGS TO PRACTICE OPEN CHORDS

"Wonderwall" by Oasis - This iconic song primarily uses open chords such as Em, G, D, and A7sus4. The strumming pattern and chord transitions are great for beginners learning to play open chords smoothly.

"Sweet Home Alabama" by Lynyrd Skynrd - This classic rock song features open chords like D, C, and G. It has a catchy rhythm and is perfect for practicing chord changes and rhythm playing.

"Horse With No Name" by America- This song is simple yet effective for practicing open chords. It mainly uses Em and D6add9/F#, making it ideal for beginners to work on chord transitions and strumming patterns.

Charts are available for these songs in many URLs, including **https://www.ultimate-guitar.com/**

Learn different **chord voicings** from there. New variations help you to add a new dynamic and flavour to your playing skills.

Chord progressions are sequences of chords, creating the musical structure of your song, establishing a tonal centre, and conveying movement and emotion.

The most common among these is the 1, 4, and 5 **progressions** (if you're in the key of c, the **progression would** be c, f, g).

Other common **progressions** are 1, 5, 6, 4, used chiefly in pop music, and 1, 2, 5, used sometimes in jazz. Add your new strumming patterns and picking techniques to this mixture, and you will become a full-fledged guitarist.

Learn to read **chord diagrams** and understand **chord symbols**, enabling you to play chords from sheet music.

Feel free to experiment with **inversions**, **substitutions**, and **new voicings**, adding variety and creating your vibe.

"The guitar is a miniature orchestra in itself." – Ludwig van Beethoven

Ludwig van Beethoven
Source – Wikimedia Common

BARRE CHORDS

Move on to 'barre' chords. Using this method, you can play **chords** in different positions on the neck. Playing this way is tricky at first, but it will become way more effortless as time passes (and callouses develop). When I was learning guitar as a child, I thought these were "Bar" chords because you use your fingers as a bar on the guitar frets to change keys.

Barre chords allow you to use one finger to press down on multiple strings across a single fret, effectively creating a movable nut. This technique allows guitarists to play chords not limited to the open position, offering a greater range of harmonic possibilities and enabling the play of chords in any key. The most common finger used to create the "barre" is the index finger, which presses down all six strings on a particular fret using the other fingers to form the chord.

When I was a boy, my older sister **Kathleen** would sit at her acoustic guitar, her lovely long blond hair falling over it, singing her originals and some folksy popular songs, moving the Barre up and down the strings for each song. I marvelled at her raw, natural talent. It was then that I realized how barre chords can change the entire vibe of a guitar from song to song. Years later, I was able to produce her two albums, filled with her lovely, intricate acoustic guitar work and angelic vocals.

Kathleen Sisler Soffer
Source – Sisler Private Collection

The two most common barre chord shapes are based on the E major and A major open chord shapes, often called the "E shape" and "A shape" barre chords. For example, you create an A major chord by placing the index finger across all the strings on the fifth fret and forming an E major shape with the remaining fingers. This same principle applies to minor chords and other variations, providing a versatile tool for playing chords up and down the neck of the guitar. Barre chords are instrumental in genres like rock, blues, and jazz, where quick key changes and complex chord progressions are common.

Learning barre chords can be challenging for beginners due to the finger strength and precision required. Still, consistent practice can help overcome these difficulties. Exercises like practicing the barre shape alone or gradually building up from more straightforward chords can be helpful. Mastery of barre chords expands a guitarist's chord vocabulary.

EXERCISES TO BUILD STRENGTH

Here are a handful of exercises to build strength for playing barre chords:

Finger Press Exercise: Place your index finger across all six strings on any fret, pressing down firmly to create a clean sound. Hold for a few seconds, then release and repeat. This exercise strengthens your index finger and helps you get used to the barre position.

Single Finger Barre: Practice barring the top two strings (high E and B) with your index finger. Once comfortable, add the next string (G), and continue until you can comfortably press down all six strings with a single finger. This step-by-step approach helps build strength gradually.

Chord Transitions: Practice switching between open chords and barre chords, such as moving from an open E major to an E-shaped barre chord on different frets. This exercise improves finger agility and helps you get used to the barre chord shape.

Spider Exercise: Place your index finger across all six strings on the fifth fret (creating a barre), and then use your other fingers to play an E major shape. Move this shape up and down the fretboard while maintaining the barre. This exercise strengthens your fingers and improves coordination.

Finger Strengtheners: Use finger strengtheners or grip trainers designed for guitarists. Squeezing these devices regularly helps build the finger and hand strength needed for pressing down barre chords.

Gradual Build-Up: Start with partial barre chords, like playing only the top three or four strings, and gradually work up to full six-string barre chords. This gradual increase helps build strength without overwhelming your fingers.

Playing Scales with Barre: Practice playing scales while maintaining a barre with your index finger. For example, play a major or minor scale up and down the neck, keeping the barre in place. This exercise improves both strength and dexterity.

SONGS TO PRACTICE BARRE CHORDS

"Hotel California" by **The Eagles** — **"Hotel California"** features numerous barre chords, particularly Bm, F#, and G. The iconic intro and verses offer an excellent opportunity to practice switching between various barre chord shapes.

"Creep" by **Radiohead** - **"Creep"** is another excellent choice for practicing barre chords. It primarily uses G, B, C, and Cm, with the B and Cm being barre chords. This song is slower, making focusing on clean transitions between chords easier.

"Shape Of My Heart" by **Sting**- This song includes a variety of barre chords and is excellent for practicing both major and minor shapes. The sophisticated chord progressions offer a good challenge for improving finger strength and positioning.

Charts are available for these songs on many sites, including **https://www.ultimate-guitar.com/**

POWER CHORDS

Power chords are the foundation for heavy metal guitar playing, and they are known for their simplicity and powerful sound. Typically, power chords consist of just two or three notes: the root note and the fifth interval, and sometimes the octave of the root. This stripped-down structure gives power chords a robust and clear sound that is less muddy than full chords, making them ideal for high-gain distortion settings often used in rock and metal music. Power chords are played using movable shapes, which means the exact finger positioning can be shifted up and down the fretboard to produce different chords, offering great flexibility and ease of use for guitarists.

Lita Ford was propelled into stardom as lead guitarist for **The Runaways**. She is one of the premier solo artists and heavy metal guitarists of the 1980s. Guitarists today should emulate her power chords and energetic solos.

Lita Ford
Credit — Wikimedia Commons

The most common power chord shape is formed when you place the index finger on the root note, using the low E or A string, and the ring finger or pinkie finger two frets higher on the adjacent string. For example, an A5 power chord would have the root note A on the fifth fret of the low E string and the E note using the seventh fret of the A string. This simplicity allows beginners to quickly incorporate power chords into their playing, even if they have yet to become comfortable with more complex chord shapes. Power chords are foundational in punk, grunge, and classic rock. They are used extensively by bands such as Nirvana, Green Day, and AC/DC, making them a critical element of a guitarist's repertoire.

BASIC POWER CHORD SHAPES

The most basic power chord shape consists of two notes: the root and the fifth. This is typically played by placing the index finger on the root note on either the low E or A string and then placing the ring finger or pinkie finger two frets higher on the adjacent string. For example, to play a G5 power chord, put your index finger firmly on the third fret of your low E string (the G note) and place your ring finger firmly on the fifth fret of the A string (the D note). This shape can be moved up and down the fretboard to play different power chords, maintaining the same relative finger positions.

A slightly more advanced power chord shape adds the octave of the root note. Using the G5 example would involve putting your pinkie finger firmly on the fifth fret of your D string and adding another G note. This creates a fuller sound while maintaining the simplicity and ease of playing that power chords are known for. These shapes are highly versatile and can be easily incorporated into many musical contexts. The movable nature of power chords means that once you learn the shape, you can play them in any key by simply shifting your hand up or down the neck of the guitar.

USING POWER CHORDS IN DIFFERENT GENRES

Power chords can be used across various musical genres due to their simplicity and powerful sound. In rock and metal, they are a staple, providing the foundation for many iconic riffs and progressions. Bands like AC/DC, Nirvana, and Green Day utilize power chords to create driving, high-energy songs with a clear, aggressive tone that cuts through the mix. Power chords are often played with heavy distortion in these genres to enhance their fullness and sustain, making them essential for creating the characteristic "wall of sound" effect. Additionally, the ease of moving power chord shapes up and down the fretboard allows for quick key changes and dynamic shifts, which is common in rock and metal compositions.

The Ramones
Credit- Wikimedia Commons

Beyond rock and metal, power chords are also used in punk, grunge, and pop music. In punk rock, power chords are essential for their raw, straightforward sound that matches the genre's rebellious and energetic spirit. Bands like **The Ramones** and **The Sex Pistols** rely heavily on power chords to drive their fast-paced, three-chord anthems. Grunge bands like **Pearl Jam** and **Soundgarden** use power chords to create a heavier, more layered sound, often combining them with intricate lead lines and dynamic shifts. In pop music, power chords can add a rock edge to otherwise clean and melodic compositions, as seen in songs by artists like **Avril Lavigne** and **Kelly Clarkson**. This adaptability makes power chords a fundamental tool for guitarists across various musical styles.

Transitioning between power chords smoothly involves several key techniques. First, ensure your hand is relaxed and natural, with your thumb resting behind the neck to provide support. When moving from one power chord to another, maintain the shape of your fingers and slide them up or down the fretboard to the next position rather than lifting them entirely off the strings. This sliding motion helps maintain contact with the strings, resulting in smoother transitions and less string noise. Additionally, practice moving between different power chords slowly, focusing on accuracy and keeping the pressure needed to produce clear notes. As you become more comfortable, gradually increase your speed. Consistent practice of these transitions using a metronome can also help improve timing and precision.

SONGS TO PRACTICE POWER CHORDS

"Smells Like Teen Spirit" by **Nirvana**- **"Teen Spirit"** heavily relies on power chords throughout its riff and chorus. It uses simple power chord shapes, making it perfect for beginners to practice transitions and maintain consistent pressure.

"Iron Man" by **Black Sabbath** - This classic metal song features powerful, heavy riffs based on power chords. The main riff is excellent for practicing slow, deliberate transitions between power chords and maintaining a robust and clean sound.

"All The Small Things" by **Blink-182**- This pop-punk hit is built around straightforward power chord progressions. Its fast tempo and catchy rhythm make it ideal for practicing quick transitions and developing a tight, rhythmic strumming pattern.

Charts are available for these songs in many spots, including https://www.ultimate-guitar.com/

EXPLORING SCALES AND MELODIES

Scales are note sequences played in ascending or descending order, providing the foundation for solos and melodies. Start by learning the **major scale** in each key and practicing it by playing it in different positions on the neck of your guitar. Then, move on to **minor scales**, natural, harmonic, and melodic. As you progress, experiment with **blues scales**, **pentatonic scales**, and different **modes** like **Dorian**, **Phrygian**, and **Mixolydian**, each evoking different emotions through its unique character.

Continue to use the knowledge of strumming, picking, and chording as you practice your scales with various **articulations and rhythms**, developing your **finger dexterity** and becoming more familiar with the fretboard. Now is the time to start chording without looking at your hand, working on the **fluidity** of your playing, and making the whole experience more natural for you. If you're wondering what **modes** are, they are scales derived from major scales. Each mode has its distinct sound and character. The **major scale** is called the **Ionian mode**... the other have variations on this mode, including **Dorian**, **lydian**, **mixolydian**, **aeolian**, **Phrygian**, and **Locrian** modes. Each **mode** leads you to characteristic **chord progressions** and **intervals**.

Later, choosing to compose your music will provide a foundation that exists in your subconscious mind. You won't even know where it's coming from, but it will be there as you learn **improvisation** and **composition**. When you learn to **improvise**, you have achieved the point where you spontaneously create music in real-time, using your knowledge of **scales** and **modes** and your **intuition** to generate solos and melodies. **Improvising** comes with **practice**, so start improvising over easy chord progressions, using modes or scales that fit the underlying harmony. Develop a **melodic sense** as you learn to express emotions through your performance.

Great techniques for improvisation include bends, slides, phrasing, vibrato, and call-and-response, adding expression and dynamics to your performance. Find recordings of great improvisers in different genres, emulating their choice of notes, phrasing, and sense of timing. All this works to expand your knowledge and style. How do you create **captivating melodies**? The **melody is** the heart of the song. **Melody** is the fundamental series of notes that leaves a lasting impression on the listener.

Return to your scales and experiment with different modes, creating **melodic phrases**. Move by adjacent notes and use larger **intervals** to create interest. Pay attention to **timing** and **rhythm**, using rhythmic variations, syncopation, and rests to enhance the appeal of your melodies.

"Don't be afraid to expand yourself, to step out of your comfort zone. That's where the joy and the adventure lie." – Herbie Hancock

Herbie Hancock
Credit: Wikimedia Commons

As you incorporate bends, arpeggios, slides, and vibrato into your **melodies, remember** to trust your ear and **intuition,** guiding you to create melodies that truly captivate your listeners while instilling a sense of self-assurance and confidence. Remember, some of the most powerful melodies are the **simplest** ones. Embrace the wisdom of the acronym K.I.S.S., which stands for "keep it simple, stupid." It's not an insult, but a reminder of the beauty and impact of simplicity in music. This knowledge empowers you to create melodies that resonate with your audience. Now, delve into the intricate art of playing and picking the guitar with your **fingers.** Using both hands to play makes you a stronger player. You can always use a pick to play whenever it's called for.

My friend, actress **Dyan Cannon** once reminded us that Shakespeare said, *"Nothing is either good or bad but thinking makes it so."* There is no right or wrong way to expand your musical prowess. It's all about how you think as an individual and how you apply your unique thoughts to the instrument.

Dyan Cannon and Tad Sisler
Source – Sisler Private Collection

FUNDAMENTAL MUSIC THEORY CONCEPTS

Although I'm not teaching a music **theory and harmony** course in this book, I strongly suggest that any musician take as many music theory and harmony courses as you can find, from beginning to advanced. The more you understand the **fundamentals** of music, the better musician you become; it's that simple.

The foundation of music theory is **notes, intervals,** and **rhythm**, which we've already discussed. Beyond this, it helps you to dive into **chord voicings, chord construction,** and **harmonies.**

My wife, **Stephanie** (God rest her soul), absolutely loved music and wanted so much to be a musician when she was here with us. **Stephanie** went to college, took music theory and harmony, and aced it, but she couldn't do it regarding **ear training**. She realized that she didn't have the natural talent that makes ear training easier, which was highly frustrating for her. Anyway, she did amazing things on the business side of music, promoting concerts and running a successful talent agency before we lost her.

What I'm leading to is that theory and harmony can only take you to a certain point, but it's all there to help you with **ear training.**

On the other hand, I have a type of **perfect pitch**, which accelerated my ear training as a kid. You can play any note on the piano, and I can tell you what it is blindfolded. The blessing of **perfect pitch** became a problem for me when keyboards included transposers. I would use the transposer to play in an 'easier' key. Still, I heard the song in the original key, which messed up my playing because I kept thinking of the original key while playing in another. Performing in one key while hearing another became a new form of ear training for me, though, learning to divorce myself from the note I was listening to and concentrate on the new key I was playing in. I mostly abandoned this later, except when it didn't fit my vocal range.

Ear **training is not just about listening and practicing**, but also about emulating the great artists who inspire you. So, dive in, immerse yourself in the world of sound, and let it guide your musical growth.

CHAPTER NINE
READING TABLATURE

G uitar tablature, or "tab," is a simplified musical notation used primarily by guitarists to read and play music easily. Unlike standard musical notation, which uses staff lines and notes, tablature represents the guitar's fretboard, indicating exactly where to place your fingers. A guitar tab consists of six horizontal lines, each representing one of the guitar's strings, with the bottom line representing the lowest (sixth) string and the top line representing the highest (first) string. Numbers placed on these lines indicate the frets that you should press. For instance, a "3" on the bottom line means you should press the third fret of the low E string.

Tabs, the heart of guitar tablature, can also include various symbols to indicate different playing techniques. For example, "h" might denote a hammer-on, "p" a pull-off, "b" a bend, and "/" a slide. These symbols provide additional guidance on how to play specific notes or passages, making tabs an expressive and detailed form of notation for guitar music. Guitar tablature is a treasure trove for beginners and self-taught guitarists. It visually demonstrates where to place fingers, bypassing the need to understand traditional musical notation. And the best part? It's widely available online for nearly any song, making it an accessible tool for learning and mastering new pieces. The world of guitar music is at your fingertips!

Guitar tablature with symbols is a slightly more advanced way of reading music for guitar compared to standard guitar chord charts. You don't have to learn tablature with symbols to become a great guitarist, but you might find later, when you are in situations where you need to be a good reader of music, this knowledge will be essential. So, keep pushing your boundaries and exploring new ways to enhance your musical skills. The rewards will be worth it!

Here are two easy chords a beginner guitarist can play using a guitar chord chart:

E Minor Chord: The E minor chord is simple and requires only two fingers.

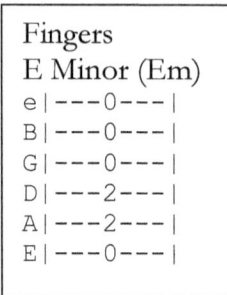

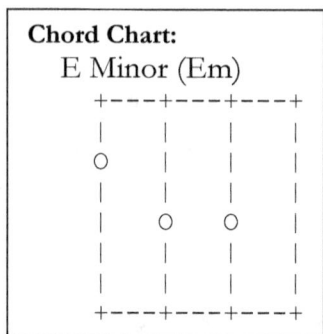

In the chord chart, the circles represent where you place your fingers. The "O" shows that you are playing an open string. For E minor, place your middle finger on the 2nd fret - A string and your ring finger on the 2nd fret - D string. All other strings are played open.

G Major Chord: The G major chord provides a fuller sound and is also beginner friendly.

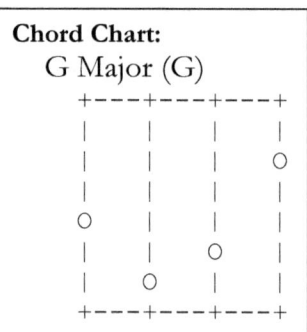

As shown in the chord chart for G major, put your middle finger on the 3rd fret - low E string. You should place your index finger on the 2nd fret - A string, and ring finger on the 3rd fret - high E string. The B and G strings are played open.

These charts help beginners visualize finger placement on the fretboard. In doing so, you will find it easier to learn and play chords.

Remember, the most important thing is to believe in yourself. It's not easy, but if you have faith in your abilities, the opinions of others become insignificant. As my dear friend **Khloe Kardashian** said:

"Stay away from those who try to diminish your aspirations. Don't let anyone dampen your spirit!"

If she can do it, so can you!

Tad Sisler with Khloe Kardashian and Robin Dougan
Source – Sisler Private Collection

For more detailed instructions and additional chords, you can refer to resources. Here are three great resources:

https://www.ultimate-guitar.com/
https://www.songsterr.com/
https://chordify.net/

UNDERSTANDING TABLATURE SYMBOLS

Guitar tablature (tab) uses various symbols to indicate different playing techniques and provide detailed instructions on how to play a song.

Reading and interpreting tablature (or "tab") may initially appear daunting for a beginner guitarist, but it's straightforward. Tablature is a musical notation designed for the guitar, offering a clear visual representation of the fretboard. The six horizontal lines in a tab correspond to the guitar's six strings. Bottom line represents the low E string (thickest string). Top line represents the high E string (thinnest string). Numbers placed on these lines indicate the frets that need to be pressed. For instance, a "3" on the bottom line means you should press the third fret of the low E string. When multiple numbers are stacked vertically, those notes should be played simultaneously, forming a chord. With some practice, you'll find that reading and interpreting guitar tablature is not as complex as it may seem initially.

In addition to the numbers, various symbols in tablature indicate different techniques. For example, "h" stands for a hammer-on, where you pick the first note and press another fret without picking again. A "p" indicates a pull-off, the opposite of a hammer-on. A "/" or "denotes a slide, moving your finger up or down the fretboard from one note to another. "b" signifies a bend, where you push the string up to raise the pitch, and "~" or "v" represents vibrato, where you rapidly bend and release the string to create a vibrating sound. "PM" or dots below the tab indicate palm muting, where you rest your palm lightly on the strings near the bridge while playing.

Example:

```
e|----------------0---|
B|------------I-------|
G|---------2----------|
D|-------2------------|
A|----0---------------|
E|--------------------|
```

In this example, you play the open A string (0), then press the second fret on the D string (2), then the second fret on the G string (2), the first fret on the B string (I), and finally the open high E string (0). This sequence forms an A minor chord. At first, these may seem highly confusing. Still, as you learn, it gets more manageable, and you can quickly glance at a tab and play it immediately. First, I suggest you know each symbol's meaning and then practice it.

EXAMPLES OF COMMON TAB SYMBOLS:

Hammer-On (h):   •Example: 5h7
•This symbol indicates that you should play the note on the 5th fret and hammer onto the 7th fret without re-picking the string.

Pull-Off (p):   •Example: 7p5
•This symbol indicates that you should play the note on the 7th fret, then pull off to the 5th fret without re-picking the string.

Slide (/) or (\):   •Example: 5/7 or 7\5
•A forward slash (/) indicates sliding up from the 5th fret to the 7th fret, while a backslash (\) indicates sliding down from the 7th to the 5th fret.

Bend (b) and Release (r):   •Example: 7b9 or 7b9r7
•This symbol indicates that you should bend the note at the 7th fret up to the pitch of the 9th fret. If followed by an "r," release the bend back to the original note.

Vibrato (~~):   •Example: 5~~
•This symbol indicates that you should apply vibrato to the note on the 5th fret, creating a slight oscillation in pitch.

Palm Muting (PM):   •Example: PM--------
•This symbol indicates that you should mute the strings with the palm of your picking hand while playing the notes.

Tapping (t):   •Example: t12p7p5
•This symbol indicates that you should tap the note on the 12th fret and then pull off to the notes on the 7th and 5th frets.

IMAGE EXAMPLES OF GUITAR TAB NOTATION:

Below is a simplified example of guitar tablature, illustrating some of the standard symbols:

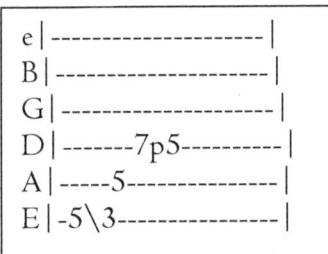

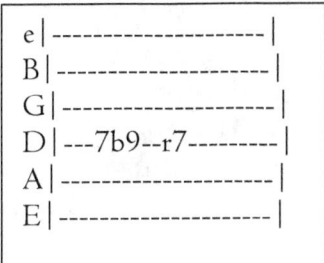

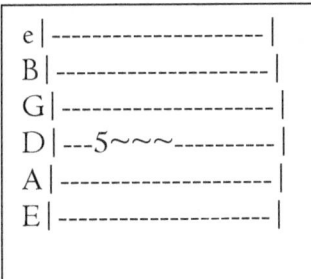

This example shows hammer-ons, pull-offs, slides, bends, vibrato, and palm muting in guitar tab notation. Each symbol provides specific instructions on playing the notes, helping guitarists accurately replicate the intended sound and technique.

For more detailed instructions and additional chords, you can refer to resources. Here are three great resources:

https://www.ultimate-guitar.com/
https://www.songsterr.com/
https://chordify.net/.

My dear friend, the great actor **Gene Barry** said:

"The attitude of the actor is his interpretation of what he reads, and the written word is what creates the role in the actor's mind."

So, basically, comparing guitar playing to acting, tablature is the "written word" that creates the 'role' of the music, and it's up to you to interpret it in your special way.

Tad, Rachel and Stephanie Sisler with Gene Barry
Source – Sisler Private Collection

BENEFITS OF LEARNING TABLATURE

Learning to read and perform music or guitar tablature is like acting. You begin to visualize the song and relay your unique interpretation of the song to your audience through your passion and attitude within your performance. Learning guitar tablature (tab) offers several significant benefits for guitarists, especially beginners:

Simplicity and Accessibility: Guitar tablature is much simpler to read than standard musical notation.

It provides a straightforward representation of where to place your fingers visually on the fretboard, making it accessible for beginners who may not have a background in reading music.

Direct Application: Tabs show precisely how a song is played, including finger placement, specific frets, and the strings you will use. Learning from tabs lets guitarists see how to use different methods like hammer-ons, pull-offs, slides, and bends in actual songs.

Wide Availability: Tablature is widely available for a vast range of songs across all genres. Many websites offer extensive libraries of tabs, often with user ratings and comments that help verify their accuracy.

Learning and Practicing Techniques: Tabs often include symbols that indicate specific guitar techniques. This feature helps guitarists learn and practice bends, slides, vibrato, and tapping in the context of actual songs.

Motivation and Enjoyment: Playing recognizable songs early in the learning process is highly motivating for beginners. Learning to play favorite songs using tabs can make practice sessions more engaging and rewarding.

PLAYING SIMPLE SONGS WITH TABS

Here are three simple songs that a guitarist can play using tabs. You can find these tabs on the reference sites we've already listed.

Deep Purple Guitarist Ritchie Blackmore
Credit-Wikimedia Commons

1.   **"Smoke on the Water" - by Deep Purple**:
"Smoke on the Water" is known for its iconic simple and repetitive riff, making it perfect for beginners. The main riff can be played on just one string, allowing new guitarists to focus on finger placement and timing.

2.   **"Horse with No Name" - by America**:
This song features a simple strumming pattern and chord progression, making it ideal for beginners. The repetitive nature of the chords helps guitarists practice smooth transitions and rhythm.

3.   **"Knockin' on Heaven's Door" - by Bob Dylan**:
This song features a straightforward chord progression and an easy strumming pattern. The simplicity of the chords allows new players to focus on their timing and transitions.

RECAP / STEP-BY-STEP GUIDE TO TABLATURE

Understand the Basics of Tablature: Tablature is a notation of six horizontal lines representing the guitar's six strings. The bottom line corresponds to the low E string (6th string), and the top line corresponds to the high E string (1st string). Numbers on these lines show which fret you should press down.

Familiarize Yourself with the Symbols: Learn the standard symbols used in tabs. For example:

- h for hammer-on
- p for pull-off
- / for slide up
- \ for slide down
- b for bend
- r for release bend
- ~ for vibrato

Read the Tab from Left to Right: Read your tabs from left to right, just like reading a book. Play each note in the order in which it appears. If multiple numbers are stacked vertically, play them simultaneously as a chord.

Start with Simple Songs: Begin with easy songs to get comfortable with reading and playing tabs. For example, start with "Smoke on the Water" by Deep Purple, "Horse with No Name" by America, or "Knockin' on Heaven's Door" by Bob Dylan.

Place Your Fingers Correctly: Follow the numbers on the tab to put your fingers on correct frets and strings. For instance, a 3 on the bottom line means you should press the third fret of the low E string.

Practice Slowly: Start playing the tab slowly, ensuring you press the correct frets and strings. Focus on accuracy before increasing your speed.

Use a Metronome: Practicing with a metronome helps maintain a steady rhythm and improves timing. Begin slowly and gradually increase your tempo as you become more comfortable with the tab.

Incorporate Techniques: As you play, apply the techniques indicated by the symbols (e.g., hammer-ons, pull-offs, slides). These techniques add expression and dynamics to your playing.

Repeat and Refine: Repeat the sections until you can play them smoothly and accurately. Focus on transitioning between notes and chords seamlessly.

Play Along with the Song: Once you feel confident, try playing with the original song to match the timing and rhythm. This exercise helps you to understand how the tab fits within the context of the music.

Example: To play the intro riff of **"Smoke on the Water"**:

```
e|-------------------------------------|
B|-------------------------------------|
G|-------------------------------------|
D|---0-3-5---0-3-6-5---0-3-5-3-0-|
A|---0-3-5---0-3-6-5---0-3-5-3-0-|
E|-------------------------------------|
```

•Put your index finger on the 3rd fret - D string and follow the sequence of numbers to play the notes accordingly.

Now, work on transitioning between tab sections. Record and review your practice as you become more familiar with tabs.

"Nobody loses at guitar if they put in the time. Something good always shows up. It's all consistent with life's big lessons. Patience. Determination. Love. Goals. Finishing a job. Etc." – Ted Greene

WRITING TABS YOURSELF

Understand the Structure: Six horizontal lines representing the guitar's six strings are the foundation of guitar tablature. The bottom line corresponds to the low E string, and the top line corresponds to the high E string. Numbers placed on these lines indicate the frets to be pressed.

Indicate Techniques: Use common symbols to indicate specific techniques:

- h for hammer-on
- p for pull-off
- / for slide up
- \ for slide down
- b for bend
- r for release bend
- ~ for vibrato
- PM for palm mute

Write Sequentially: Write the tablature from left to right, placing numbers where you want to play the notes. Ensure that chords (notes played simultaneously) are aligned vertically.

Add Timing and Rhythms: Use spacing or additional symbols to indicate the timing and rhythm of the notes. While tablature typically does not convey rhythm as precisely as standard notation, using spaces and symbols like | for bar lines can help.

TOOLS AND SOFTWARE FOR WRITING TABS

1.   **Guitar Pro**: Guitar Pro is comprehensive for writing, playing, and sharing tabs. This website features tools for notating music and adding various playing techniques.
   - https://www.guitar-pro.com/
2.   **Ultimate Guitar Tab Editor**: This website is an online tool provided by **Ultimate Guitar** that allows you to write and share your tabs directly on their platform.
   - https://www.ultimate-guitar.com/
3.   **TablEdit** is a software program for creating, editing, listening, and printing sheet music and tablature for guitar and other instruments.
   - https://tabledit.com/

EXERCISES TO PRACTICE WRITING TABS

Transcribe Simple Songs: Start by writing tabs for simple songs or riffs that you know well. This practice helps familiarize you with the tab notation and improves your transcription skills.

Create Original Riffs: Write tabs for your original riffs and chord progressions. This exercise encourages creativity and helps you understand how to notate different techniques.

Transcribe Solos: Challenge yourself by transcribing guitar solos. Pay attention to the nuances of the performance, including bends, slides, and vibrato.

SHARING TABS WITH OTHERS

Online Communities: Share your tabs on websites like **Ultimate Guitar** or **Songsterr,** where other musicians can view and rate your work.
   - https://www.ultimate-guitar.com/
   - https://www.songsterr.com/

Social Media: Engage with your community using platforms like YouTube, Instagram, or Facebook to share videos or images of your tabs for valuable feedback.

Personal Website or Blog: Create your own website or start a blog to share your tabs, tips, and tutorials to help you build a following and connect with other musicians.

BENEFITS OF WRITING YOUR OWN TABS

Enhanced Learning: Writing your own tabs reinforces your understanding of musical structure and guitar techniques, leading to more profound musical knowledge.

Improved Ear Training: Transcribing songs and solos improves your ability to recognize notes and intervals by ear, a crucial skill for any musician.

Creativity and Originality: Creating and notating music yourself encourages creativity and helps you develop a unique style.

Sharing Knowledge: Sharing your tabs with others can help fellow guitarists learn new songs and techniques, fostering community and collaboration.

CHAPTER TEN
RHYTHM AND TIMING
THE HEARTBEAT OF MUSIC

"Most beginners want to learn lead because they think it's cool.
Consequently, they never really develop good rhythm skills. Since most of
a rock guitarists time is spent playing rhythm, it's important to learn to do
it well. Learning lead should come after you can play solid backup and
have the sound of the chords in your head."
— Eddie Van Halen

Van Halen with Sammy Hagar
Credit – Wikimedia Commons

Our brains are hardwired to respond to rhythmic patterns, making rhythm a vital element in perceiving and enjoying music. Studies have shown that rhythm activates multiple brain areas involved in motor control, timing, and auditory processing, leading to the synchronization of neural activities. This synchronization can evoke strong emotional responses, improve cognitive functions, and enhance social bonding. Remarkably, rhythm's influence extends beyond music, as rhythmic patterns are integral to human speech and language development, underscoring rhythm's fundamental role in human communication and cognition.

Legendary **Guns 'N Roses** guitarist **Slash** sees the guitar as a form of communication that goes beyond verbal expression, encouraging us to explore the guitars potential as a language of its own.

"The guitar has this magical ability to convey what words alone can't. It's
like a language of its own, and I'm addicted to speaking it." - Slash

Slash
Credit – Wikimedia Commons

UNDERSTANDING RHYTHM

Rhythm is the foundation of music, dictating the timing and flow of a piece, maintaining the groove and ensuring that your playing meshes well with other instruments. The basics of rhythm include understanding time signatures, beat divisions, and different strumming or picking patterns.

Time Signatures:
•**4/4 Time**: 4/4 is the most common time signature, indicating four beats in a measure and a quarter note for each beat. It's often referred to as "common time."
•**3/4 Time**: Waltzes are played in 3/4 time, indicating three beats per measure and a quarter note for each beat.
•**6/8 Time**: 6/8 time is often found in ballads and folk music, where there are six eighth notes per measure, grouped in twos or threes.

Types of Rhythms:
•**Straight Rhythm**: Notes or chords are played evenly, directly on the beat.
•**Syncopated Rhythm**: Accents are placed on beats or parts of beats that are usually not accented, creating a more complex and interesting rhythm.
•**Shuffle/Swing Rhythm**: Notes are played in a long-short pattern, giving a "swinging" feel often found in jazz and blues.

EXERCISES TO PRACTICE RHYTHM

Metronome Practice: Use a metronome to practice strumming or picking on different beats. Start with 4/4 time, playing a downstroke on each beat. Gradually increase the tempo as you become more comfortable.

Clapping Rhythms: Clap out different rhythms before playing them on the guitar. This exercise helps internalize the rhythm without worrying about finger placement.

Strumming Patterns: Practice common strumming patterns, such as:
• Down-Up-Down-Up (D U D U) for straight rhythms.
• Down-Down-Up-Up-Down-Up (D D U U D U) for more syncopated rhythms.

Playing Along with Drum Tracks: Use drum tracks or backing tracks to practice keeping time and fitting your guitar playing within a rhythmic context.

Subdivision Practice: Practice playing quarter, eighth, and sixteenth notes with a metronome. Start with one strum per beat (quarter notes), then two strums per beat (eighth notes), and finally four strums per beat (sixteenth notes).

Accenting Exercises: Practice strumming patterns where you accent different beats. For example, accent the first and third beats in a 4/4 measure, then switch to accenting the second and fourth beats.

Syncopation Practice: Work on playing syncopated rhythms by shifting the accents to off-beats. Start with simple syncopated patterns and gradually increase complexity as you improve.

EXAMPLES OF RHYTHM IN POPULAR SONGS
I.   "Back in Black" by AC/DC:
This song features a robust, driving rhythm guitar part fundamental to its iconic sound. The rhythm guitar plays simple yet effective power chords and palm-muted riffs that create a tight, punchy groove. The consistent downstroke strumming adds to the song's intensity and energy.

2. **"Sweet Child O' Mine" by Guns N' Roses:**

While known for its famous lead guitar riff, "Sweet Child O' Mine" also has a solid rhythm guitar part that provides the backbone for the song. The rhythm guitar uses open and barre chords with a syncopated strumming pattern, adding depth and texture to the overall arrangement.

3. **"Wonderwall" by Oasis:**

This song is an excellent example of rhythm guitar in a pop-rock context. The strumming pattern combines downstrokes and upstrokes, creating a rhythmic, flowing feel that drives the song. Using capo on the second fret and simple chord shapes makes it accessible for beginners while still effective.

Guns N' Roses
Credit – Wikimedia Commons

COUNTING BEATS AND MEASURES

Beats: Beats are the fundamental units of time in music. In most Western music, beats are evenly spaced and form the backbone of the musical timing. You can divide each beat into smaller subdivisions, such as half beats (eighth notes) or quarter beats (sixteenth notes). The tempo of a piece of music, usually measured in beats per minute (BPM), indicates how fast or slow these beats occur. For example, a tempo of 60 BPM means you have one beat per second, while a tempo of 120 BPM means two beats per second.

Measures (Bars): Measures, also known as bars, are segments of time defined by a given number of beats, separated by vertical lines on the staff in standard musical notation. The time signature at the beginning of a piece of music tells you beats per measured and type of note. As mentioned above, 4/4 indicates four beats in each measure, with a quarter note receiving one beat. Measures help organize the music into manageable chunks, making reading, writing, and playing more functional.

Practical Example: In a 4/4 time signature, each measure consists of four beats. When strumming chords in a song, you might count out loud "1, 2, 3, 4" for each measure, with each count corresponding to a beat. If you are playing a song at 120 BPM, each beat (or count) happens twice per second, creating a steady rhythm to follow.

COUNTING IN DIFFERENT TIME SIGNATURES

Understanding Time Signatures: Time signatures indicate how many beats are in each measure and what type of note receives one beat. We write them as a fraction. The top number shows the number of beats per measure. The bottom number indicates the note value per one beat.

Common Time Signatures:
4/4 Time Signature:
•Also known as "common time," it is Western music's most widely used time signature.
•Counting: "1, 2, 3, 4"
•Example: Most pop, rock, and blues songs.
Practice strumming a simple chord on each beat, emphasizing the first beat of each measure to internalize the downbeat.

3/4 Time Signature:
•Often referred to as "waltz time," it has three beats per measure.
•Counting: "1, 2, 3"
•Example: "Amazing Grace" and many waltz tunes.
Practice playing a chord on the first beat and lightly strumming the successive two beats to emphasize the waltz feel.

6/8 Time Signature:
•Common in ballads and folk music, it has six beats per measure, emphasizing the first and fourth beats.
•Counting: "1, 2, 3, 4, 5, 6"
•Example: "House of the Rising Sun" by The Animals.
Play a chord on the first and fourth beats to feel the compound rhythm, often divided into two groups of three.

2/4 Time Signature:
•Known as "march time," it has two beats per measure.
•Counting: "1, 2"
•Example: "When the Saints Go Marching In."
Practice alternating between a bass note on the first beat and a chord on the second to simulate a marching rhythm.

5/4 Time Signature:
•Less common and often used in progressive rock or jazz, it has five beats per measure.

•Counting: "1, 2, 3, 4, 5"
•Example: "Take Five" by Dave Brubeck.

Break it into smaller groups (e.g., 3+2 or 2+3) to make counting more effortless, and practice strumming patterns that fit these groupings.

EXERCISES TO PRACTICE DIFFERENT TIME SIGNATURES

Metronome Practice: Use a metronome set to different time signatures. Many digital metronomes and apps allow you to set custom time signatures.

Clapping and Counting: Clap along with the metronome while counting out loud to internalize the rhythm. Start with simple time signatures like 4/4 and 3/4 before moving to more complex ones like 5/4 and 7/8.

Song Practice: Play songs written in various time signatures to get used to switching between them. For example, try playing "Norwegian Wood" by The Beatles (in 6/8) and "Money" by Pink Floyd (in 7/4).

Writing Rhythms: Write your own rhythms in different time signatures. Start with basic strumming patterns and gradually add more complexity as you become comfortable. Remember the online resources we've mentioned for tablature.

IMPORTANCE OF KEEPING TIME

Keeping time ensures that you stay in sync with other instruments and maintain the overall groove and structure of the music. Good timing allows for more expressive and dynamic playing, improving your ability to play accurately, enhancing your musicality, and making you a more reliable and versatile musician.

EXERCISES FOR PRACTICING COUNTING AND KEEPING TIME

I've learned that when I'm performing songs with unusual time signatures, I should count to myself as I'm playing so I don't get lost. You've already done many of these exercises for different reasons.

You'll find that exercises like metronome practice help in myriad ways. This time, we'll show some of the same exercises with a different focus:

Metronome Practice: Set a metronome to a slow tempo (e.g., 60 BPM) and practice playing a single chord or note on each beat. Gradually increase the tempo as you become more comfortable. Practice playing on different beat subdivisions (e.g., quarter notes, eighth notes, sixteenth notes).

Clap and Count: Clap along with a metronome while counting the beats out loud. Start with simple time signatures like 4/4 and gradually move to more complex ones like 5/4 or 7/8. Clap different rhythmic patterns while keeping the count steady. For example, clap on a measure's first and third beats and then switch to clapping on the second and fourth beats.

Subdivision Drills: Practice strumming or picking exercises that emphasize different beat subdivisions. For instance, alternate between playing quarter notes, eighth notes, and triplets within a single measure. Combine different subdivisions within a measure to create more complex rhythms.

Rhythmic Reading: Use rhythm reading exercises to practice playing specific rhythmic patterns. Clap or play these patterns on your guitar while following along with written notation or tabs.

Play Along with Drum Tracks: Use drum tracks or backing tracks to practice keeping time. Focus on locking in with the drummer's beat and maintaining a consistent rhythm.

Recording Yourself: Record yourself playing along with a metronome or backing track. Listen back to check if you are staying in time and adjust as necessary. Record different rhythmic patterns and play them back to analyze your timing and consistency.

USING A METRONOME

I've mentioned metronomes all over the place in a few chapters. When I performed for years poolside at all the hotels in the Palm Desert, California, area, I used a drum machine that works like a metronome to help you develop an inner timing. When you're away from it after a certain point, you begin to know when you're rushing or slowing down.

• Choose a metronome: Decide between a mechanical, electronic, or app-based metronome (keyboard with built-in BPM or drum sequencers work, too) based on your preference.

- Set the BPM: Determine the tempo you want to practice at. For beginners, start with a slower tempo (e.g., 60 BPM) and gradually increase as you become more comfortable.
- Turn on the metronome and listen to the clicks or beats.
- Play with the metronome, ensuring each note or chord aligns with the beat. Start by playing a single note or chord on each beat.
- Gradually incorporate more complex rhythms and subdivisions, such as eighth notes, triplets, and sixteenth notes, while maintaining alignment with the metronome.

BENEFITS OF USING A METRONOME

A metronome helps improve timing, ensuring you play evenly and consistently, which is crucial for playing with other musicians. Practicing with a metronome allows you to control and maintain a steady tempo, preventing unintentional speeding up or slowing down during a performance. It aids in developing technical precision by ensuring that complex passages and rhythms are played accurately and evenly.

EXERCISES TO PRACTICE WITH A METRONOME

Single Note Exercise: Play a single note or open string on each beat of the metronome. Start slow. Gradually increase your tempo as you become more comfortable.

Chord Changes: Practice changing between chords on each beat. Begin with simple chords and a slow tempo, then increase the speed and complexity as you improve.

Subdivision Practice: Play quarter notes, eighth notes, triplets, and sixteenth notes to a single metronome beat. This exercise helps in understanding and executing different rhythmic subdivisions.

Scales and Arpeggios: Practice scales and arpeggios with the metronome, starting slowly and focusing on clean, even playing. Gradually increase your tempo as your accuracy improves.

Syncopation and Complex Rhythms: Incorporate syncopated rhythms and off-beat patterns into your practice to develop a more advanced sense of timing and rhythm.

INCORPORATE METRONOME PRACTICE INTO YOUR ROUTINE in every practice session, even for a few minutes. Consistent use reinforces timing and rhythm skills over time. Vary the exercises and tempos to challenge different aspects of your playing. Mix slow, precise practice with faster, more challenging tempos. Integrate metronome practice into your repertoire work.

Use it to practice difficult passages, ensuring you can play them accurately at a steady tempo. Keep a practice journal, noting tempos and specific exercises. Gradually increase the tempo as you achieve mastery at each level.

CHAPTER ELEVEN
DEVELOPING TIMING AND COORDINATION
PLAYING ALONG WITH BACKGROUND TRACKS

A few of my friends firmly believe you aren't a musician if you use backing tracks. Truthfully, you do need to learn to play proficiently without backing. Still, in today's world, you need to have as many available resources as possible to help you succeed.

Using backing tracks is an excellent way for guitarists to enhance practice sessions and simulate playing with a full band. Backing tracks provide a pre-recorded accompaniment that includes instruments such as drums, bass, keyboards, and sometimes rhythm guitar. This backing allows you to focus on lead playing, improvisation, or rhythm parts in a more dynamic and engaging context, developing timing, phrasing, and musicality, making it a fantastic tool for beginners and advanced players.

FINDING AND CHOOSING BACKING TRACKS

Online Platforms: Websites like **Jam Tracks, YouTube**, and **Ultimate Guitar** offer various backing tracks in different genres and styles. These platforms often provide tracks of varying complexity, catering to different skill levels.

Music Apps: Apps like **iRealPro** and **AmpliTube** offer customizable backing tracks where users can change the key, tempo, and instrumentation to suit their practice needs.

Genres and Styles: Choose backing tracks that align with your musical interests and goals. For example, if you enjoy blues, look for backing tracks featuring 12-bar blues progressions. Find tracks with standard jazz progressions like ii-V-I if you're into jazz.

EXERCISES TO PRACTICE WITH TRACKS

Scales and Improvisation: Play with the backing track using scales that fit the track's key. Practice improvising solos and focus on creating melodies that complement the harmony.

Chord Changes: Practice switching between chords in time with the backing track. This exercise helps improve your rhythm playing and ensures you can keep up with the tempo.

Phrasing and Dynamics: Work on your phrasing by playing short, melodic lines and paying attention to how they interact with the backing track. Experiment with dynamics, such as playing softly in certain sections and louder in others.

Rhythm Practice: Use backing tracks to practice strumming and picking patterns. Match your rhythm to the track's groove, ensuring tight synchronization with the beat.

"The song tells me what to play." – Joe Walsh

Joe Walsh
Source - Wikipedia

BENEFITS OF PLAYING WITH RHYTHM TRACKS

Playing with backing tracks helps you develop a strong sense of timing and rhythm, as you must stay in sync with the accompaniment. Backing tracks provide a more musical and enjoyable practice experience. They help you learn how to interact musically with other instruments and improve your musicianship.

Practicing with tracks in different styles and genres broadens your musical horizons and enhances your versatility as a guitarist. Backing tracks simulate a live band environment, making them excellent for performance preparation. They allow you to practice your parts within the context of a full arrangement.

COORDINATING YOUR HANDS

Effective coordination between both hands ensures that the left hand can press down the correct frets. In contrast, the right hand simultaneously picks or strums the proper strings. Good hand coordination leads to cleaner, more precise playing, allowing for smoother transitions between chords, scales, and techniques. It also minimizes unwanted noises, such as string buzz or missed notes.

HAND COORDINATION EXERCISES

Spider Exercise: Place your fingers on the first four frets of the low E string, starting with the index finger on the first fret. Play each note sequentially, moving up the strings while maintaining proper finger placement. This exercise helps synchronize the movements of both hands.

Finger Independence Exercise: Practice tapping each finger individually on a flat surface or the guitar neck, ensuring the other fingers remain relaxed. This exercise builds finger strength and independence, crucial for smooth coordination.

String Skipping Exercise: Play notes on non-adjacent strings while maintaining a steady rhythm. For example, play the first fret on the low E string, then the second fret on the D string, and so on. This exercise enhances accuracy and coordination between both hands.

COMMON COORDINATION ISSUES

String Buzz: Ensure that your left-hand fingers press close to the fret, not in the middle. Also, apply adequate pressure to avoid buzzing.

Missed Notes: Slow down your practice tempo and focus on precise finger placement and picking technique. Gradually increase the speed as accuracy improves.

Inconsistent Rhythm: Practice with a metronome to develop a steady sense of timing. Focus on synchronizing your hand movements with the metronome clicks.

PLAYING SCALES TO IMPROVE COORDINATION is an effective way to improve hand coordination. Begin with simple scales like the major or minor scales and play them slowly, ensuring each note is clear and precise. Gradually increase the tempo as you become more comfortable. Focus on keeping both hands synchronized and maintaining consistent finger placement.

PRACTICE CHORD TRANSITIONS TO IMPROVE YOUR COORDINATION, changing from one chord to another smoothly and accurately. Start with basic chord progressions, such as G-C-D or E-A-B, and practice switching between them slowly.

Ensure that your fingers move simultaneously and that each chord rings out clearly. Using a metronome helps you to maintain a steady rhythm. As you become more proficient, increase the tempo and incorporate more complex chord progressions into your practice routine.

SYNCOPATION AND ADVANCED RHYTHMS

From a drummer's perspective, **Ringo Starr** highlighted the unique nature of syncopation in his playing by saying:

"My occupation is syncopation. But every time, my syncopation is different, because I can never play the same fill twice. I just can't, never have been able to."

Ringo Starr
Credit – Wikimedia Commons

Syncopation is the deliberate disruption of the regular flow of rhythm, creating an unexpected accent or emphasis on beats or parts of beats that are typically not accented. This technique adds complexity and excitement to music, often making it more dynamic and engaging. For guitarists, mastering syncopation involves understanding how to place these off-beat accents and integrating them smoothly into their playing. Syncopation can be used in various genres, including jazz, funk, rock, and classical, adding a layer of rhythmic sophistication to the music.

TYPES OF SYNCOPATION

Off-Beat Syncopation: We place accents on the weaker beats or the "ands" between the main beats. For example, in a 4/4-time signature, the emphasis might be on the "and" of 2 or 4.

114

Suspended Syncopation: This exercise involves holding a note across the strong beat into the next weak beat, creating a sense of suspension and release, and, for example, playing a note on the "and" of 2 and holding it into beat 3.

Anticipated Syncopation: Accents occur just before the strong beat, creating a sense of anticipation and, for example, playing on the "and" of 4 leading into beat I of the next measure.

EXERCISES TO PRACTICE SYNCOPATION

Clapping and Counting: Clap along with a metronome, emphasizing the off-beats or weaker beats. Count out loud and practice placing accents on different parts of the measure.

Rhythmic Variations: Take a simple chord progression and practice strumming with syncopated rhythms. Start with basic off-beat accents and gradually incorporate more complex syncopated patterns.

Listening and Imitation: Listen to music known for its syncopation, such as jazz or funk. Try replicating the syncopated rhythms on your guitar by playing with the recordings.

INCORPORATING SYNCOPATION

Start Simple: Begin by incorporating simple off-beat accents into your strumming or picking patterns. Focus on maintaining a steady underlying rhythm while adding syncopated accents.

Gradual Complexity: Gradually introduce more complex syncopated patterns, such as anticipated or suspended syncopation. Practice these patterns in different musical contexts to develop versatility.

Improvisation: Use syncopation in your improvisations to create interesting rhythmic variations. Experiment with different placements of accents to see how they change the feel of your solos.

BENEFITS OF MASTERING SYNCOPATION

Enhanced Musicality: Syncopation adds depth and interest to your playing, making your music more engaging and expressive.

Improved Rhythmic Flexibility: Mastering syncopation improves your ability to navigate complex rhythms, enhancing your overall rhythmic proficiency.

Versatility Across Genres: Syncopation is used in many musical styles, from jazz and funk to rock and classical.

Being proficient in syncopation allows you to adapt your playing to a wide range of genres.

Creative Expression: Syncopation provides a tool for creative expression. Syncopation allows you to experiment with rhythmic patterns and create unique musical phrases.

CHAPTER TWELVE
APPLYING RHYTHM TO SONGS

SELECTING RHYTHM FOCUSED SONGS

W hen selecting rhythm-focused songs, look for tracks with clear and distinctive strumming or picking patterns that emphasize rhythmic elements. Songs with straightforward chord progressions and repetitive rhythmic structures are ideal for practicing and improving rhythm skills. Genres like rock, pop, blues, and folk often feature prominent rhythm guitar parts that can serve as excellent practice material. Also, choosing songs you enjoy and are familiar with can make the practice process more engaging and motivating.

BREAKING DOWN RHYTHM PATTERNS

To effectively practice rhythm, start by listening closely to the chosen song and identifying the main rhythmic patterns. Pay attention to the strumming or picking techniques, the tempo, and the time signature. Use a metronome to match the song's tempo and practice tapping out the rhythm before playing it on the guitar. Break the song into verses, choruses, and bridges, and focus on mastering each part individually. Write down or use guitar tablature and chord charts to visualize the rhythmic patterns and chord changes.

PRACTICING RHYTHM WITH SIMPLE SONGS

Begin practicing with simple songs that have basic chord progressions and steady rhythms. Songs like *"Knockin' on Heaven's Door"* by **Bob Dylan**, *"Wonderwall"* by **Oasis**, and *"Sweet Home Alabama"* by **Lynyrd Skynyrd** are great examples.

Start by slowly strumming along to the song, ensuring each strum aligns with the beat. Gradually increase the tempo as you become more comfortable. Focus on maintaining smooth transitions between chords with a consistent rhythm.

Example Exercise with "Wonderwall" by Oasis
1.   **Identify the Rhythm Pattern:**
The main strumming pattern for "Wonderwall" is often written as D-DU-UDU (Down, Down, Up, Up, Down, Up).
2.   **Break it Down:**
Practice the strumming pattern slowly without worrying about the chords. Focus on getting the rhythm right.
3.   **Incorporate Chords:**
Once comfortable with the strumming pattern, add the chords. For "Wonderwall," the primary chords are Em7, G, Dsus4, and A7sus4.
4.   **Practice with a Metronome:**

Use a metronome set to a slow tempo.

Strum along with the metronome to ensure your timing is consistent.

5. **Play Along with the Song**:

After mastering the rhythm and chords separately, play along with the original recording to match the song's tempo and feel.

BENEFITS OF RHYTHM FOCUSED PRACTICE

Practicing rhythm-focused songs enhances your timing, coordination, and ability to play in sync with other musicians. It builds a solid rhythmic foundation, critical for rhythm and lead guitar playing.

CREATING YOUR UNIQUE RHYTHM PATTERNS

"Rhythm is something you either have or don't have, but when you have it, you have it all over." – Elvis Presley

Elvis Presley
Credit - Wikimedia Commons via Picryl.com

Creating rhythm patterns involves understanding the fundamental elements of rhythm, such as time signatures, beat subdivisions, and strumming or picking techniques. Start by choosing a time signature, like 4/4 or 3/4, which will dictate the structure of your rhythm pattern. Next, decide on the beat subdivisions you want to use, such as quarter notes, eighth notes, or sixteenth notes. Experiment with downstrokes and upstrokes in different combinations to develop a natural strumming pattern that suits the musical context. Incorporating syncopation, where accents fall on off-beats or weaker beats, can add complexity and interest to your rhythm patterns.

TOOLS AND EXTENSIONS FOR PRACTICING

Metronome: Using a metronome helps you to maintain a steady tempo while experimenting with different rhythm patterns.

Rhythm Notation Software: Tools like **Guitar Pro, TuxGuitar**, and online rhythm generators can help you visualize and notate your rhythm patterns.

Clapping and Counting: Internalize the rhythm, practicing clapping out your rhythm patterns while counting the beats aloud.

Recording Yourself: Record your rhythm patterns and listen back to evaluate the consistency and feel.

Wireless System: Several years ago, I went to a **Rolling Stones** concert at a huge outdoor stadium in San Diego, California. It was raining heavily that night, and the rain did not deter the **Stones** at all! They slid across the stage playing their guitars with wireless systems! It was cool! A wireless guitar system provides greater freedom of movement on stage, allowing you to perform more dynamically without being tethered to a cable, and reduces the risk of tripping over cords, accidental unplugging, and the tangling of cables, which can interrupt a performance. Additionally, wireless systems can improve stage aesthetics by eliminating clutter and providing a cleaner setup. They usually feature high-quality sound transmission that maintains the integrity of the guitar's tone, and many modern systems offer reliable signal strength and minimal latency, making them suitable for both live performances and rehearsals.

INCORPORATING RHYTHM INTO SONGS

Once you have created a rhythm pattern, the next step is to integrate it into a song. Start by applying your pattern to a simple chord progression, ensuring each chord change aligns with the rhythm. Practice playing the entire progression with your rhythm pattern, maintaining a steady tempo and smooth transitions between chords. Gradually incorporate more complex patterns and syncopation as you become more confident.

Additionally, adapt your rhythm patterns to verses, choruses, and bridges to add variety and dynamics.

BENEFITS OF CREATING UNIQUE RHYTHMS

Taking the initiative to create unique rhythms enhances your understanding of rhythm and timing, making you a more versatile and creative musician. Custom rhythms can add a distinctive touch to your music, setting your playing apart. It also improves your ability to adapt to different musical contexts, whether you're playing solo, in a band, or accompanying a vocalist.

PLAYING IN THE POCKET

Playing "in the pocket" is one of the most important things you should learn as a guitarist. Pocket playing involves maintaining a steady rhythm and perfectly syncing with your rhythm section, particularly the bass and drums. This ability ensures tight and cohesive performances and enhances the music's overall groove and feel. Playing in the pocket allows you to build a solid foundation to add expressive elements, like dynamics and embellishments, while maintaining the integrity of the song's rhythmic structure. It is especially important in genres like funk, R&B, and jazz, where groove and rhythm are central to the music's feel. Many garage band musicians don't realize that they would instantly sound more professional if they learned to play in the pocket together. Some of my favorite 'pocket' guitarists over the years have ben **Al McKay, Johnny Graham, Jimmy Nolen, Catfish Collins,** and my friends **Craig T. Cooper** and **Morris O'Connor,** all worthy of you taking the time to study their styles.

The benefits of playing in the pocket extend beyond musical cohesion. It demonstrates your proficiency and sensitivity to the ensemble's needs, making you a more versatile and desirable collaborator. Being able to lock in with other musicians creates a more compelling and engaging performance for the audience, as the music feels more natural and fluid. Additionally, mastering this skill helps you develop better timing, listening skills, and overall musicianship.

COLLABORATION WITH OTHER MUSICIANS
Collaborating with other musicians exposes you to different playing styles, techniques, and musical perspectives, helping you develop better timing, rhythm, and listening skills, as you need to stay in sync and complement the other instruments. Collaboration also encourages creativity and inspiration.

FINDING MUSICIANS WHO COLLABORATE
Local Music Schools and Workshops: Enroll in music classes or workshops to meet other musicians with similar interests.
Open Mic Nights and Jam Sessions: Attend local open mic nights and jam sessions to connect with other musicians in a casual setting.
Online Platforms: Use online platforms like **BandMix, JamKazam**, and social media groups dedicated to musicians looking to collaborate.
Music Stores and Community Boards: Check community boards at local music stores for collaboration opportunities and musician classifieds.
Music Apps: Apps like **Vampr** and **Jammcard** help musicians connect based on location, genre, and skill level.

EXERCISES TO PRACTICE COLLABORATING
Jamming: Regularly jam with other musicians, focusing on improvisation and spontaneous musical interaction. Performing with others helps develop your ability to adapt and respond to different musical ideas.
Cover Songs: Practice playing cover songs together, considering how each instrument contributes to the overall arrangement. This exercise improves coordination and timing.

Songwriting Sessions: Collaborate on songwriting sessions where each musician contributes ideas. Collaboration fosters creativity and teamwork and helps you learn how to blend different musical elements.

Recording Projects: Working on recording projects with other musicians requires precise coordination and communication. This exercise enhances your technical skills and understanding of production processes.

Jennifer Batten, one of the great collaborating guitarists of the 1990s, played lead guitar for **Michael Jackson** during his *Bad* and *Dangerous* tours.   Her innovative use of effects and her technical prowess places her in a league of her own among masters of rock guitar.

Jennifer Batten
Credit – Wikimedia Commons

LEARNING RECORDING TECHNIQUES

"The guitar has an incredible range of tones and textures, and it allows me to create landscapes of sound. It's a journey every time I pick it up." –
David Gilmour

In the studio, regardless of the music genre, I've discovered that establishing a foundation, which often includes rhythm guitar, is imperative. Rhythm guitar players employ a range of techniques and styles on recordings, depending on the genre and the desired sound. Here are a few common styles:

Chicken Picking: A hybrid picking style often used in country and rock, where the guitarist uses a pick for downstrokes and fingers for plucking, creating a "clucking" sound. It is popular in country and blues recordings.

Fast Strumming: This technique involves quick, rhythmic strumming across the strings, often seen in rock, punk, and folk genres, to create energy and drive within a song.

Palm Muting: By lightly placing the side of the picking hand on the strings near the bridge, guitarists dampen the strings to create a tight, percussive sound, frequently used in rock and metal for rhythmic clarity and heaviness.

Funk Strumming: Also known as "choppy" or "percussive" strumming, this style is characterized by tight, syncopated rhythms, often with muted strings between the chords, creating a funky, groove-based feel.

Arpeggiated Chords: This style involves picking the individual notes of a chord in sequence rather than strumming all the notes at once. It's commonly used in genres like folk, pop, and indie rock for a more delicate, melodic feel.

Power Chords: Often used in rock and punk, power chords are played using only two or three strings, typically focusing on the root and fifth, to create a complete, aggressive sound.

These styles, with their unique characteristics, can be mixed and adapted to fit different genres, showcasing the flexibility and open-mindedness that rhythm guitar can bring to the rhythm section of a song.

BENEFITS OF PLAYING WITH OTHERS

Enhanced Musical Skills: Playing with others improves your technical abilities, timing, and rhythm, as you must synchronize with the group.

Broadened Musical Horizons: Exposure to different genres, styles, and techniques expands your musical knowledge and versatility.

Creativity and Inspiration: Collaborating with other musicians sparks new ideas and inspires creativity, leading to more innovative and dynamic music.

Networking Opportunities: Building relationships with other musicians brings new opportunities, including gigs, recordings, and collaborations on future projects.

Improved Listening and Communication: Playing with others enhances your listening skills and ability to communicate musically, which is essential for successful collaborations.

SINGING WHILE PLAYING GUITAR

If you can sing and play guitar, you become much more valuable when collaborating with other musicians. Researching other musicians who play and sing will also help your learning experience. **George Benson** famously sang to his intricate guitar solos, doubling each note with his voice. **Peter Frampton** used a talk box to change his vocal sound, an effects device that modulated his voice to sound synthy. He was an accomplished guitar player who could play, sing, and project on stage without his instrument. **Stevie Wonder** often used a vocoder, adding an electronic texture to his vocals. The French electronic duo

Daft Punk frequently uses vocoder and auto-tune to create their futuristic sound.

"The fun for me in collaboration is, one, working with other people just makes you smarter; that's proven.
— Lin-Manuel Miranda

Lin-Manuel Miranda
Credit — Wikimedia Commons

EXPAND YOUR REPERTOIRE

I've been learning new songs regularly throughout my entire career. My repertoire consists of around 3,000 songs, close to the **Guinness World Record** if I perform them all back-to-back.

I promised myself when I was younger that I would do my best to keep up with music trends and technology. Staying current is essential today if you don't want to be left behind.

Learn songs! Learn by ear, reading charts, using chord charts, working with other musicians, watching videos, listening, rehearsing, and practicing. The more you play the songs, the more they become ingrained in you.

I've trained myself to remember songs I haven't played in ten or more years. However, memory is limited; sometimes, I can't remember what I did when I woke up this morning!

I also promised myself when I was younger that I would do my best to embrace all forms of music, which can be a challenge sometimes when I hear some of the music people are putting out today!

My grandfather, **Theodore Witt,** said,

"The house of music has many rooms, including the outhouse!"

It's improbable to embrace all forms of music based on one's particular tastes. Still, it would help if you explored as many genres as possible, including rock, jazz, folk, blues, classical, urban, and R&B. Broaden your musical horizons. You will become a more rounded individual, not to mention a monster player. My favorite guitarists may be jazz virtuosos or classical gods. Still, they can play a sustained rock solo as good or better than any great rock guitarist. By doing so, you will become more rounded and more in demand.

I had a friend who had recently graduated from **Berklee.** He was possibly the fastest jazz guitarist I ever met and was at the ripe age of 22. I hired him to do gigs with the band, but I found that as studied as he was, he was one-dimensional. When I needed a rock solo on *"Johnny B. Goode,"* he sounded like **John McLaughlin** or **Julian Lage**, playing the fastest jazz solo I've heard in years. I'm not saying the solo wasn't amazing; it just did not match the song or the moment.

You may unleash your unique originality and creativity as you grow by composing music and lyrics. Composing music and writing lyrics are by far the most rewarding of all the things I've done musically.

Never think that finding your groove or strength is like finding a needle in a haystack. It's there, I promise you, ready to be revealed.

My friend, actor **Lorenzo Lamas** said:

"Most haystacks do not even have a needle."

Tad Sisler with Lorenzo Lamas and A.J. Lamas
Source- Sisler Private Collection

CHAPTER THIRTEEN
ADVANCED TECHNIQUES
LEAD AND RHYTHM GUITAR

Let's look at the critical differences between rhythm guitar and lead guitar, and how their roles and techniques vary in a band setting: The key differences between rhythm guitar and lead guitar are their roles, techniques, and contributions to a band's overall sound.

RHYTHM GUITAR: The primary role of the rhythm guitarist is to provide the harmonic foundation and maintain the groove of the song.

Rhythmic guitar playing involves chords and strumming patterns that complement the bass and drums, creating a cohesive backing for the lead instruments and vocals. Rhythm guitarists ensure that the song's structure and timing remain solid.

Rhythm Guitar Techniques: Rhythm guitarists typically use strumming, palm muting, and arpeggios. They often play power, barre, and open chords to provide a rich harmonic backdrop. Rhythm guitarists frequently practice with a metronome to maintain steady tempos.

Contributions to the Band: Rhythm Guitar contributes to the song's overall rhythm and harmony, ensuring a stable foundation. It fills out the sound, making the music feel complete and cohesive. Rhythm guitar is often the backbone of the song, supporting other instruments.

LEAD GUITAR: The lead guitarist focuses on playing melodies, riffs, solos, and embellishments that stand out from the rhythm section. Their role is to add expressiveness and complexity to the music, often taking center stage during instrumental breaks and solos. Lead guitarists frequently use bends, slides, vibrato, and tapping techniques to create dynamic and intricate musical lines.

Lead Guitar Techniques: Lead guitarists employ various techniques to enhance their solos and melodies. These include bending notes, hammer-ons, pull-offs, slides, vibrato, and tapping. Mastery of scales and modes is crucial for improvisation and soloing, allowing lead guitarists to navigate the fretboard fluidly and creatively.

Contributions to the Band: Lead Guitar adds melodic interest and highlights moments through solos and intricate riffs. The lead guitar's contributions often provide the song's memorable hooks and showcase the guitarist's technical prowess. Lead parts are usually more prominent in the mix, capturing the listener's attention.

IMPORTANCE OF FINGERPICKING
Fingerpicking enhances your versatility and ability to create rich, layered sounds.

It enables players to produce a more nuanced and dynamic performance, with greater control over each note's volume and articulation. This technique also expands your repertoire, allowing you to tackle a broader range of musical styles and compositions. **Ana Popovic** utilizes many of these techniques in her performances. Born in Serbia, Ana greatly impacted the international blues scene with her passionate, fiery guitar work. She blends blues with rock, funk, and jazz. She's dynamic and worthy of you studying and analyzing her playing.

Ana Popovic
Credit – Wikimedia Commons

BASIC FINGERPICKING PATTERNS

Alternating Thumb Pattern: The thumb alternates between two or three bass strings. The fingers play the higher strings. For example, in a 4/4 time signature, the thumb might alternate between the 6th and 4th strings while the index and middle fingers pluck the 3rd and 2nd strings.

Travis Picking: As I've already described, this pattern involves a steady bass rhythm played by the thumb. At the same time, the fingers pick out a syncopated melody on the higher strings. A typical pattern is thumb (T) on the 6th string, index (I) on the 3rd string, thumb on the 4th string, and middle (M) on the 2nd string.

Arpeggio Pattern: Play the notes of a chord in sequence, typically from the lowest to the highest string. For example, in a C major chord, you might pluck the 5th string with the thumb, the 4th string with the index, the 3rd string with the middle, and the 2nd string with the ring finger.

EXERCISES TO PRACTICE FINGERPICKING

Single Chord Pattern: Choose a simple chord like C major or G major, and practice a basic fingerpicking pattern. Focus on keeping the rhythm steady and the notes clear.

Alternating Thumb: Practice alternating the thumb between different bass strings while maintaining a steady rhythm. Use a metronome to help keep time.

Travis Picking Exercise: Work slowly on the Travis picking pattern, ensuring each note is clean and precise. Gradually increase the tempo as you become more comfortable.

Arpeggios: Practice playing arpeggios across different chords, focusing on smooth transitions and consistent finger placement.

FINGERPICKING WITH DIFFERENT GENRES

Folk: Often uses simple, repetitive patterns that emphasize melody and harmony. Songs like *"Blackbird"* by **The Beatles** feature iconic fingerpicking patterns. For an exercise in Folk, look to the guitar work of **Woodie Guthrie, Bob Dylan,** and **Joan Baez.**

Classical: Involves complex, precise patterns that require a high level of skill and control.

Pieces by composers like Bach and Tarrega are fundamental to classical fingerpicking.

Blues: Combines fingerpicking with slides, bends, and other techniques to create expressive, soulful music. Blues fingerpicking often emphasizes syncopation and groove.

Country: Utilizes Travis picking and other patterns to create a driving rhythm and melodic lines. Country songs often blend fingerpicking with strumming for a fuller sound.

"Approach your guitar intelligently, and if there are limits, don't deny them. Work within your restrictions. Some things you can do better than others, some things you can't do as well. So, accentuate the positive."
— Chet Atkins

Chet Atkins
Credit - Wikimedia Commons via Picryl.com

BENEFITS OF MASTERING FINGERPICKING

Increased Versatility: Mastering fingerpicking allows you to play a broader range of music, from classical to modern acoustic styles.

Enhanced Musicality: Fingerpicking provides greater control over dynamics and articulation, leading to more expressive and nuanced playing.

Improved Coordination: Fingerpicking exercises develop finger independence and coordination, essential skills for any guitarist.

Expanded Repertoire: Fingerpicking opens many songs and pieces that rely on this technique, enriching your musical library.

ADVANCED FINGERPICKING TECHNIQUES

Advanced fingerpicking patterns involve more complex rhythms, intricate techniques, and greater coordination between the fingers of the picking hand. These patterns allow guitarists to play more elaborate and expressive pieces, incorporating multiple musical lines simultaneously.

Percussive Fingerstyle: This technique combines fingerpicking with percussive elements, such as tapping the guitar's body or slapping the strings to create rhythmic accents. Artists like **Andy McKee** and **Jon Gomm** are known for using percussive fingerstyle.

Thumb Independence: Advanced patterns often require the thumb to maintain a steady bass line while the fingers play independent melodies or harmonies. This technique is essential in styles like ragtime and certain forms of blues.

Harp Harmonics: This technique involves producing harmonic notes by lightly touching the string at specific points while plucking. It creates a bell-like, ethereal sound often used in classical and modern fingerstyle pieces.

Cross-String Picking: This technique involves alternating fingers across different strings to play rapid sequences of notes, creating a smooth, flowing sound commonly used in classical guitar and complex fingerstyle arrangements.

EXERCISES TO IMPROVE ADVANCED PATTERNS

Travis Picking Variations: Practice Travis picking with different chord progressions and incorporate syncopation. Start with the basic pattern and gradually add variations, such as hammer-ons, pull-offs, and slides.

Percussive Techniques: Incorporate percussive elements into your practice by tapping the guitar body or strings between notes. Practice combining these percussive hits with regular fingerpicking to create a cohesive rhythm.

Thumb Independence Exercises: Work on exercises that separate the thumb's movement from the other fingers. For example, play a steady bass line with your thumb while practicing different finger patterns on the higher strings.

Harp Harmonics Practice: Practice playing harmonics at various points along the fretboard. Combine these harmonics with fingerpicked notes to create layered, harmonic-rich passages.

"Every day I'm getting shaped and molded. Keepin' on, being a better artist, and improving on this, improving on that. The more I'm in it, the more I'm practicing and the more I'm advancing." – Lil' Baby

Lil Baby
Credit – Wikimedia Commons

INCORPORATING ADVANCED PATTERNS

Identify Suitable Songs: Choose songs that naturally lend themselves to advanced fingerpicking, such as pieces by **Michael Hedges, Leo Kottke,** or **Tommy Emmanuel**. These artists often use complex fingerpicking patterns in their compositions.

Adapt Existing Songs: Take more straightforward songs and add advanced fingerpicking elements to them. For example, add percussive hits or harmonic flourishes to enhance the arrangement.

Compose Your Own Pieces: Use advanced fingerpicking techniques to compose original pieces. Experiment with patterns, rhythms, and techniques to create unique and expressive music.

CONTINUING SKILL DEVELOPMENT

This last section is a recap of the most important elements I've outlined in this book to give you what you need to excel and succeed.

First and foremost, embrace your mistakes. Mistakes are part of the process. Frustration holds you back, so relax and take deep breaths as you learn and improve! Developing proficiency and mastery in playing the guitar involves a progressive journey from basic to advanced techniques, driven by passion, dedication, and structured practice. Practice consistently with a metronome, using simple songs, and engage in exercises that improve finger independence are crucial at this stage.

"I taught myself how to play the guitar, so I basically learned by a system of making mistakes." – Richie Sambora

Richie Sambora
Credit – Wikimedia Commons

The desire for mastery goes beyond technical skills; it encompasses musicality, creativity, and personal expression. A master can execute complex techniques flawlessly, playing with emotion, phrasing, and dynamics that captivate listeners. Continuous learning, taking lessons, attending workshops, and playing with other musicians contribute to ongoing growth. Master guitarists often emphasize the importance of practicing intentionally, setting specific goals, and continually seeking feedback to refine their skills. Mastery is a lifelong journey, where the guitar becomes an extension of your musical voice. Mastery allows you to create and share your unique sound with the world at the highest level.

ESSENTIAL AI-POWERED APPS

Keep up with new developments in artificial intelligence. The world is changing so fast that new resources we never dreamed of come to fruition faster than we can write about. Remember, though, the basics never change. Technique, skill, and emotional performance should always be your focus. Here are some of the most popular AI-powered apps (at the time I'm writing this book) you can use to practice, expand your repertoire, perform, and record:

Yousician is an interactive app that uses AI to provide real-time feedback on guitar playing, making it a great tool for practicing and improving technique. It offers lessons and exercises for different skill levels, from beginner to advanced. **Yousician** listens to your playing through the microphone and provides instant feedback on pitch, timing, and accuracy. Guitarists can use

Yousician to practice scales, chords, and strumming patterns and even learn complete songs with guidance. It also includes challenges and weekly goals to keep players motivated.

Moises.ai is a music practice app that allows guitarists to separate instruments from songs, adjust pitch and tempo, and create custom backing tracks. Guitarists can use the app to isolate guitar tracks for learning, create karaoke-style tracks for performance, and slow down difficult sections of songs. It also allows changing the song key to match your vocal range or playing style. It is ideal for learning new songs, practicing with backing tracks, or preparing for performances.

Jamstick is a guitar-learning app with a smart guitar or MIDI controller that tracks finger placement and technique. It helps beginners learn the basics of guitar while providing feedback. Jamstick offers interactive lessons and practice exercises that guide users through chords, scales, and basic techniques. The app also includes many songs to play along with. This app is excellent for beginners who want to learn guitar in a structured and engaging way.

Amplitube is a virtual guitar amplifier and effects processor that emulates a variety of amps, cabinets, and effects, allowing guitarists to record and perform with a wide range of tones. The app provides a customizable setup where you can choose different amps, pedals, and microphone setups. It helps record guitar tracks, practice with different tones, or perform live using an audio interface. This app is perfect for guitarists experimenting with tones, recording professional-quality tracks, or enhancing their live performances with various effects.

Tonebridge Guitar Effects is a guitar effects app that provides preset tones from thousands of popular songs. It allows guitarists to recreate the sound of their favorite tracks easily. Users can search for songs and instantly apply the corresponding tone. Tonebridge provides effects settings that match the original song's guitar sound.

This app is great for guitarists who want to play along with popular songs and achieve the same tone as the original recordings.

Chordify is an AI-powered app that generates chord charts for any song. Guitarists can use it to learn and practice new songs by following chord progressions. The app analyzes songs from YouTube, Spotify, or uploaded audio files and provides real-time chord charts. It also includes tempo control and looping features for practicing tricky sections. This app is perfect for learning songs quickly by following the generated chord progressions and practicing along with the original track.

LANDR is an AI-powered mastering and distribution tool that helps guitarists enhance the quality of their recordings. It offers automated mastering, allowing users to polish their guitar recordings. LANDR also provides distribution services to upload your music to streaming platforms like Spotify and Apple Music. Guitarists who record their music can use LANDR to create professional-quality mastered tracks and share them with the world.

Guitar Pro is a guitar tablature editor software with an AI-powered transcription feature. Guitarists can create, edit, and share tablature. The software can also import existing music files and provide detailed feedback on timing, notes, and finger placement. Use Guitar Pro to transcribe guitar solos, compose original music, or practice with visual feedback on sheet music and tabs.

AI-Powered Loopers (e.g., Endlesss): Endlesss is an AI-powered looping app that allows guitarists to create loops and collaborate with other musicians in real-time. It provides an easy-to-use looping interface and AI-generated effects. The app allows you to create multiple layers of sound and jam with others from anywhere. These apps are great for improvisation practice, songwriting, or collaborating with other musicians remotely.

BUILDING CONFIDENCE AS A GUITARIST

"Confidence is the most beautiful thing you can possess."
– Sabrina Carpenter

Sabrina Carpenter
Credit – Wikimedia Commons

Building confidence stems from a solid foundation of skills, consistent training, and positive reinforcement. Recording practice sessions and noting progress over time can provide tangible evidence of improvement, further reinforcing self-assurance.

Performing for others, whether in private settings like family gatherings or public venues such as open mic nights, is a transformative experience that significantly enhances confidence. Remember everything I've mentioned about conquering stage fright and building your confidence as an artist.

Confidence in playing and performing is not just about technical proficiency but also about self-belief and enjoyment of the music. Celebrating small victories, staying patient with the learning process, and maintaining a positive attitude contribute to building lasting confidence.

Legendary **Queen** guitarist **Brian May** believed that the guitar can be a source of comfort and confidence, helping musicians express themselves when words fail.

"The guitar was my weapon, my shield to hide behind." – Brian May

Brian May
Credit- Wikimedia Commons

I WANT TO OFFER YOU A FREE GIFT

I hope you're loving this book so far. Learning an instrument can be daunting, but the rewards are exponential as you learn and grow your performance skills. I've created a list of **TEN SECRETS A MUSICIAN CANNOT LIVE WITHOUT,** and I want to share it with you.

If you want a free copy of my list, email us at...
<<   modernrenaissancepublishing@gmail.com   >>
with the subject line **TEN SECRETS FREE LIST,** and I'll email you back a free copy at no obligation whatsoever to you as a heartfelt thanks for reading this book.

CREATIVE EXPRESSION FOR A GUITARIST

Creative expression allows you to communicate emotions, tell stories, and explore their artistic identity. The desire to express oneself creatively through music often drives guitarists to learn, compose, and improvise. This journey involves not only technical skill but also an understanding of musical theory and structure, which provides a foundation for creativity.

Composing music allows guitarists to translate their emotions and experiences into melodies and harmonies. It provides a way to experiment with different musical elements, such as rhythm, dynamics, and timbre, to create a distinctive sound. Improvisation, on the other hand, offers a more spontaneous form of expression. It challenges guitarists to think on their feet and respond to the musical moment, often leading to unexpected and exciting results. Improvising helps develop a deep connection with the instrument and a more intuitive understanding of music.

AVOIDING STEREOTYPES

In all my music mastery books, I urge the reader to reject stereotypes. The most important thing you can do is what you don't do! Throughout my life, I've encountered people who bought into the negative stereotypes about musicians. When I mentioned that I was a musician, I would get a look from someone who immediately judged me as a loser. It's sad, but you will do all of us a favor if you exemplify yourself as a professional and never exhibit any of these negative stereotypes. My old friend, former championship-winning *NFL* Quarterback, **Congressman and Secretary of Housing & Urban Development Jack Kemp** talked about it in a unique way. He said:

"Winning is like shaving – you do it every day, or you wind up looking like a bum."

Tad Sisler with Congressman Jack Kemp
Source – Sisler Private Collection

It's all about the way you carry yourself, with pride and self-respect. People will pick up on your attitudes, emotions, and habits. Be the best version of yourself always and avoid these stereotypes:

Musicians are Unreliable and Irresponsible – People often stereotype musicians as flaky, unreliable, and irresponsible, particularly regarding commitments and punctuality. I will immediately write anyone off my call list who can't regularly show up on time with suitable instruments and clothing for the gig.

Substance Abuse – There is a pervasive stereotype that musicians are prone to drug and alcohol abuse, often glamorized in media and popular culture.

Financial Instability – Although this is something we cannot always control when we commit to this industry, unfortunately, many people stereotype musicians as struggling financially, living paycheck to paycheck, or unable to support themselves through their music alone. One of my friends who regularly comes to my gig has a running joke with me. He'll say, "You're good. Have you considered doing this for a living?" And I'll say, "No, it doesn't pay enough!" Everyone laughs, but the sad truth is that many musicians are grossly underpaid for their talents.

Lack of Practical Skills – Musicians are sometimes viewed as lacking practical or marketable skills outside of their music, contributing to the idea that they have few career options.

Ego and Arrogance – Musicians, especially successful ones, are often stereotyped as having big egos or arrogant, believing they are superior because of their talent. I've worked with many excellent musicians who were impossible to work with. We sounded great on stage together, but the whole experience was not worth it because of their egos or negativity. Always try to enjoy the experience and let go!

Unconventional Lifestyle – There is a stereotype that musicians lead unconventional or chaotic lifestyles with irregular hours, frequent travel, and unstable relationships.

Emotional Instability – People sometimes judge as emotionally unstable or overly sensitive, with intense mood swings or dramatic behaviour.

Promiscuity – Particularly in rock and pop culture, musicians are often stereotyped as promiscuous and engaging in numerous short-term relationships. Groupies don't help erase this stereotype!

Non-Conformity – People often see musicians as rebels or non-conformists who reject societal norms and conventional careers.

Lack of Formal Education – There's a stereotype that musicians are less formally educated or lack academic achievements, focusing solely on their craft.

These stereotypes are not universally true and can be harmful, as they overlook many musicians' diversity, dedication, and professionalism. I must admit, though, that I've often told people I'm a composer, producer, author, entertainer, or many other titles (all true) besides musician. Help propel us all forward by going against the stereotype!

CLUB, RESTAURANT, AND HOTEL GIGS

If you become proficient at playing solo guitar, you can quickly get gigs playing background music at restaurants, coffee houses, and hotels. Weddings and private events always hire solo guitarists for ceremonies and receptions. If you can sing, that's a massive plus for solo performers. I know a dozen great performers who do **"Jimmy Buffet"** style solos playing *Yacht Rock-type* music at clubs, making money and tips. If you are a classical player, you can get an upscale gig at hotels in major cities. Bands can do well in nightclubs, bars, and casinos if they play popular music, sound good, and don't take long breaks. Don't think you can play only original music unless you're working for free or paying to play in a venue where music industry executives come in to see new talent. It's great to throw in originals wherever you play, but people are there to hear familiar songs, at least until you become famous! Remember to always go against stereotypes and be a professional, and you're bound to succeed.

A few years ago, I read an article about performers trying to get their first gigs without experience. If someone happens to ask for a resume, you can put down that you've been showcasing and freelancing, studying to perfect your performance. A few of my friends have offered to come in and play for free for two hours to see if they are a good fit. Don't give up. There is a venue somewhere out there that wants you!

CORPORATE AND PRIVATE EVENTS

Performing at corporate events, private parties, weddings, and special occasions as a soloist or with a band can be a lucrative way to make money on a full-time basis. Agencies, companies, and individuals hire musicians to provide live entertainment for their events, offering not just opportunities for paid performances but also networking with potential collaborators and clients. When I started out doing this, I hooked up with an agent who controlled the corporate entertainment of several of the large hotels and convention centers in my area. Because of the number of conventions that were booked on a regular basis, I was able to quit my regular gig and work full-time doing corporate and private parties. It was a lot of setting up and breaking down my equipment, but every night was a different vibe, and I worked many day events as well. The financial security and variety of opportunities are truly rewarding.

HOW TO HANDLE PRIVATE EVENTS

Create a checklist of all equipment, instruments, wires, stands, microphones, speakers, computers, and anything else you need for the gig. You don't want to show up without an essential instrument or stand. Eventually, you'll only need a mental checklist. After breaking down our equipment at the end of each gig, we do what we call the "idiot check," going back and checking around and under the stage for anything we might have missed.

Hide your wires and equipment bags, making the stage look neat and organized. Use gig bags or cases for transporting your equipment so it does not look scratched and ugly on stage.

Show up extremely early. Showing up early, long before the event, will **calm the meeting planner** and give you plenty of time to set up your equipment to work through unforeseen issues. Also, people arrive early, so be in place and ready to perform at least 15 minutes before your scheduled start time.

Watch your volume, especially during cocktail hours and dinner sets when people like to talk.

Always look your best. Grooming and proper dress are essential for corporate gigs. Be accommodating and classy. Attitudes and emotions power everything you do. Do not eat food or drink alcohol unless the client specifically approves it.

Choose appropriate music for the moment always. Don't take long breaks unless it fits within the client's schedule. I was working a nightclub gig with a trio in **Palm Springs,** and it was an extremely slow night, so we took an exceptionally long break. My saxophonist **Pat Rizzo** looked at me and said, *"We'd better go back and play. It's almost time for our next break!"* I loved that joke, but I promise you that clients and bar owners always look at the time and expect you to take regular breaks. Most musicians play sets of 45 minutes to an hour. The usual break time is fifteen minutes. I've done nights where the client asked in advance for continuous music without breaks, and that's what they get from me. I charged accordingly.

Whatever you do, continually expand your horizons, and never stop learning. My biggest challenge in these times is keeping up with technological advances and staying current. Still, ultimately, making it all boils down to talent and persistence. My dear friend, iconic actor **Elliott Gould** believed strongly in persistence when he said:

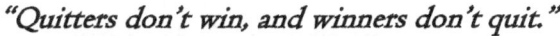

"Quitters don't win, and winners don't quit."

Tad Sisler and Elliott Gould
Source – Sisler Private Collection

CONCLUSION

Becoming an exceptional guitarist requires dedication, practice, and a commitment to continuous improvement. To unleash our inner guitar virtuoso, using the techniques of the Masters can help us to gain a positively fair advantage in our journey. As you implement these techniques, remember your unique talent is a gift to be nurtured and shared.

Above all, the most important thing to remember is to do your very best every time you perform to move your audience emotionally and connect as deeply as you can through eye contact, personality or magnetism, and a sound that people will love to hear repeatedly.

No matter what you learn from a book or mentor, nothing compares to going out and performing as often as possible. **Experience is the greatest teacher.** So, let us embark together on this transformative journey, armed with the wisdom of the masters, as we strive to become extraordinary performers and touch the hearts of all who will listen!

PLEASE LEAVE A REVIEW

Now that you have everything you need to **excel in playing guitar**, it's time to share your newfound knowledge and show other readers where they can find the same guidance.

Simply by leaving your honest opinion of this book on Amazon or wherever you purchased it, you'll help other **guitarists** discover the information they're looking for and pass their passion for **playing music** forward.
Thank you for your help. The **passion for playing guitar** is kept alive when we pass on our knowledge – and you're helping **me** to do just that.

If you purchased my book on Amazon, here's the link to leave your review:

https://www.amazon.com/review/review-your-purchases/?asin=1966258011

Or, you can just use this QR code to access the review page on Amazon:

Thanks*!!!*

ABOUT THE AUTHOR

Tad Sisler is an American Composer, Author and Producer of feature films and music. More than a thousand of his original works are available through *iTunes, Amazon* and virtually every other major marketplace. Through the years, **Tad** created and released independent feature films and documentaries, television shows, developed a music store and vast collection of music for film and television usages, in addition to published screenplays and books. **Tad** is a voting member of *The Academy of Recording Arts & Sciences.* **Tad** invented a wireless karaoke all-in-one microphone that became a best-seller on *Amazon.* A child prodigy, Tad was playing advanced piano pieces at the age of 8, and rating superior in Classical piano competitions at 12. Tad won his first scholarship for singing at 12, attending the Idyllwild School of Music and the Arts, then affiliated with the University of Southern California.

FEATURE FILMS
Tad produced, edited, and released "**The Ghosts of Brewer Town**", a mystery feature film, currently available on *YouTube.*
TELEVISION PROJECTS
Tad launched the **Journey To An Extraordinary Life-Legends Among Us** documentary series, which chronicles the lives and careers of legendary artists, actors, sports figures and heroes of medicine, in a feature-film format.

BOOKS

Books, Audio Books and Podcasts released by **Tad** include **"Reflections in the Key of Life-The Steve Madaio Story"**, chronicling the life and times of America's most prolific trumpeter. This book garnered a **Readers' Favorite Book Award** for Tad.

"Mafia Baby" is a shocking true story of a woman raped by a Mafioso, who then raised his child alone. Tad's autobiography, **"It's a Long Climb to The Middle"** *is* available currently on *Amazon* and *Barnes & Noble*. Screenplays in development by Tad Sisler include **"The Incredible Spark of Franklin Benjamin"**, and **"Please Don't Forget"**. **Tad's** latest **Music Mastery** collection of books is designed to educate and inspire musicians to become masters.

MUSIC

Tad's production music catalog tripled in size with the addition of thousands of excellent production music tracks, as well as hundreds of sound-alike tracks for the DJ/Karaoke industry, now distributed on **iTunes, Amazon Marketplace, CD Baby, Spotify, Rdio, Xbox Music** and dozens of other outlets Worldwide. **Tad** produced and released "The Barcelona Sessions" to 1000 radio stations Worldwide, with never- before-heard original performances by Miles Davis' bassist, Bill Evan's drummer, Frank Sinatra's saxophonist, Maynard Ferguson's guitarist, and Andrae Crouch' flutist/saxophonist, produced by Tad Sisler in his recording studio.

Tad Sisler composed the full score to **"The Encore Of Tony Duran"**, an indie feature film starring **Elliott Gould, William Katt, Nicki Ziering and Cody Kasch**, along with his co- composer Andrew Fraga, Jr. After having the distinction of being the first film to sell-out at the prestigious *Palm Springs International Film Festival*, the film won the **Jury Award** for **Best Feature Film** at the *Las Vegas Film Festival* and the *Santa Fe Film Festival*, as well as the **Indie Spirit Award** at the *Fort Lauderdale Film Festival* and the **Audience Favorite Award** at *Tallgrass Film Festival*, in conjunction with a **Lifetime Achievement Award** for **Elliott Gould**. The film is available on *Amazon Prime*.

Tad completed the music and audio editing for the TV Series **"American M.C."**. The first 7 episodes are complete and in the process of distribution through **iTunes**. Tad scored the Main Title theme to **American M.C.** as well as underscore and providing Music Supervision and source music.

PRODUCTION

Tad Sisler has been a valuable member of the team of specialists and project developers for **Yamaha Corporation of America**, delivering hundreds of intricate projects to exact **Yamaha** specifications over a 10 year period.

Tad received accolades in 2011 after being given the honor and challenge of doing the "official" remake of the iconic **"Andy Griffith Theme"** for the estate of the composer **Earle Hagen** as a perfect sound-alike, along with his composing associate Andrew Fraga, Jr.

Following a stint composing for a series entitled **"Famous Families"** on **Foxstar** and working as assistant to composer Jeff Edwards on the television series **"Silk Stalkings"** and **"Renegade"** in the late 1990's, Tad Sisler and founded & developed a production music catalog, containing thousands of high-quality music tracks available for sync licenses in film, television and advertising in more than 150 genres.

In addition to handling Music Supervision on **"The Encore Of Tony Duran"**, and on **"American M.C."**, **"The Ghosts of Brewer Town"**, **"Tis' The Season"**, the **"Journey To an Extraordinary Life"** series, **Tad** produced the **"It's Everyone Else Who Has A Problem!"** series, and placed his original music on **NBC, ABC/Disney, Warner Brothers Television, TNT**, US National Infomercial campaigns through **Guthy/Renker** and **Script To Screen**, as well as custom composing for the TV and Advertising industry. **Tad** released contains hundreds of top-quality soundalike tracks produced by **Tad** and his associates, for DJ and Karaoke usages, currently on *ITunes, Amazon Marketplace, Spotify, Rdio, Xbox Music,* and many other outlets.

LIVE PRODUCTION

In the 1980's and 1990's, **Tad** and his team produced a series of live headliner events at multiple venues from the ground up, including sold-out performances by **Kenny Rogers, Earth, Wind & Fire, Los Lobos, Glen Campbell, The Righteous Brothers, Lou Rawls, Tito Puente,** the **Power Jam** featuring **Timmy T, Tara Kemp, Candyman, Soul To Soul** and more.

HISTORY

As a very young man, Tad Sisler worked as a performer for **Frank Sinatra**, studied music in choreography under world-famous Broadway Dancer/Choreographer **Jacque D'Amboise**, received superior ratings in classical piano performance in tough **Joanna Hodges** international competitions, and received private acting lessons from **Richard Burton**, a friend of his family.

Tad attended the prestigious **Idyllwild School of Music and the Arts** on vocal music scholarships during the period when it was affiliated with the **University of Southern California**. In High School, Tad was one of 100 statewide vocalists elected to the prestigious **All-State Choir** in Missouri.

During his storied career, Tad has also had the honor of performing with and working among such greats as **Gladys Knight, Rita Coolidge, B.B. King, Marilyn McCoo, Johnny Mathis, Kenny Rogers, Tito Puente, Sonny and Mary Bono, Gene Barry, Teri Cole Whittaker, Shecky Greene, Peter Marshall, Mary Hart, Blackwell, Herb Jeffries, Trini Lopez, Glen Campbell, Jennifer Hudson** and other legends. Tad Sisler's extensive experience, state of the art facility and history of delivering quality feature films and music <u>on time and on budget</u>, as well as the ability to draw from an extensive catalog of production music, allows his experienced team to offer complete services in custom film and television production as well as in music composition and production efficiently.

Tad is proud and humbled to be a voting member of the **Academy of Recording Arts & Sciences**, which allows him to have a voice to vote for great artists worthy of winning a **Grammy Award**. Many of Tad's works have been placed into Grammy consideration.

In 2023, Tad won a prestigious **Telly Award** for creative excellence in his *Journey to an Extraordinary Life* film series.

Modern Renaissance Publishing is at the forefront of a new intellectual awakening, dedicated to fostering a renaissance of ideas that resonate in today's world. Our mission is to bring cutting-edge concepts and timeless wisdom to the public through a diverse array of publishing formats, including books, eBooks, and audiobooks. We are proud to launch our **Music Mastery** series, offering comprehensive guides and insights for musicians of all levels. In addition to our literary endeavors, we also publish original music, enriching the cultural landscape with creative expressions. Whether you're seeking to expand your knowledge, enhance your skills, or simply be inspired, **Modern Renaissance Publishing** provides the resources and content to empower your journey. Join us as we bridge the rich heritage of the past with the innovative spirit of the present to shape a brighter, more enlightened future.

REFERENCES

License link to all Wikimedia Commons and Creative Commons photo credit references: Creative Commons. (n.d.). *Attribution-ShareAlike 4.0 International (CC BY-SA 4.0)* [License]. Retrieved from **https://creativecommons.org/licenses/by-sa/4.0/**

Beliefnet. (2015). *Most inspirational of 2015: B.B. King.* Retrieved from **https://www.beliefnet.com/inspiration/articles/most-inspirational-of-2015-b-b-king.aspx**

Lopez, T. (n.d.). *Quote on perseverance. BrainyQuote.* Retrieved from **https://www.brainyquote.com/quotes/trini_lopez_825415**

Goodreads. (n.d.). *George H.W. Bush quotes.* Retrieved from **https://www.goodreads.com/author/quotes/579816.George_H_W_Bush**

80 Amazing Guitar Quotes and Captions for Instagram. (n.d.). *QuotesChecker.* Retrieved from **https://quoteschecker.com/guitar-quotes-and-captions/**

Guitar Quotes. (n.d.). *QuoteFancy.* Retrieved from **https://quotefancy.com/guitar-quotes**

Guitar Mammoth. (n.d.). *How many people play guitar?* Retrieved from **https://guitarmammoth.com/how-many-people-play-guitar/**

Biography.com Editors. (n.d.). *Les Paul.* Biography. Retrieved from **https://www.biography.com/musicians/les-paul**

Breakthrough Guitar. (n.d.). *How many people in the world play guitar?* Retrieved from **https://breakthroughguitar.com/how-many-people-in-the-world-play-guitar/**

King, B.B. (n.d.). *The blues was like that problem child. AtomicQuote.* Retrieved from **https://atomicquote.com/author/b-b-king/quote/the-blues-was-like-that-problem-child**

GuitarWorld. (n.d.). Retrieved from **https://www.guitarworld.com/**

Sweetwater. (n.d.). Retrieved from **https://www.sweetwater.com/**

Midder Music. (n.d.). *Guitar sales statistics*. Retrieved from **https://middermusic.com/guitar-sales-statistics/**

Breakthrough Guitar. (n.d.). *From pandemic to profit: The guitar sales growth 2023 statistics that will blow your mind*. Retrieved from **https://breakthroughguitar.com/from-pandemic-to-profit-the-guitar-sales-growth-2023-statistics-that-will-blow-your-mind/**

Santana, C. (n.d.). *Quote on music and life*. AZ Quotes. Retrieved from **https://www.azquotes.com/author/12974-Carlos_Santana**

Flack, S. (n.d.). *Second Grade Archives - Steve Flack Guitar Academy*. Retrieved from **https://steveflackguitaracademy.com/category/second-grade/**

Campaign. (2017). *Hear, hear*. Campaign, (n.d.), 31.

To Live in a Safer World. (2014). Retrieved from **https://core.ac.uk/download/324260057.pdf**

Salt Spring Coffee. (n.d.). *All the world is a birthday cake, so take a piece, but not too much – George Harrison*. Retrieved from **https://www.saltspringcoffee.com/blogs/news/all-the-world-is-a-birthday-cake-so-take-a-piece-but-not-too-much-george-harrison**

StatusBuzz. (n.d.). *Best guitar captions & quotes for Instagram*. Retrieved from **https://www.statusbuzz.in/web-stories/best-guitar-captions-quotes-for-instagram/**

Powell, C. (n.d.). *Quote on leadership*. AZ Quotes. Retrieved from **https://www.azquotes.com/author/11823-Colin_Powell**

Guitar Center. (n.d.). Retrieved from **https://www.guitarcenter.com/**

MusicRadar. (n.d.). Retrieved from **https://www.musicradar.com/**

Glen Campbell Quotes. (n.d.). *BrainyQuote*. Retrieved from **https://www.brainyquote.com/search_results?x=27&y=13&q=glen+campbell**

Moore, M. T. (n.d.). *Quote on positivity*. AZ Quotes. Retrieved from **https://www.azquotes.com/author/10341-Mary_Tyler_Moore**

Hanna, A. (2023). *Indianapolis Business Journal*. Indianapolis Business Journal, 44(14), 15B.

Hoffman, T. (n.d.). *Quote on perseverance*. AZ Quotes. Retrieved from **https://www.azquotes.com/author/26493-Trevor_Hoffman**

Motivation and Love. (n.d.). *The journey of a thousand miles begins with a single step quotes*. Retrieved from **https://motivationandlove.com/the-journey-of-a-thousand-miles-begins-with-a-single-step-quotes**

MusicianWave. (n.d.). *Guitar quotes*. Retrieved from **https://www.musicianwave.com/guitar-quotes/**

Medley, B. (n.d.). *Quote on music*. BrainyQuote. Retrieved from **https://www.brainyquote.com/authors/bill-medley-quotes**

Beethoven quotes. (n.d.). *AZ Quotes*. Retrieved from **https://www.azquotes.com/author/1135-Ludwig_van_Beethoven#google_vignette**

Cannon, D. (n.d.). *Quote on life*. AZ Quotes. Retrieved from **https://www.azquotes.com/author/2412-Dyan_Cannon**

Kardashian, K. (n.d.). *Quote on resilience*. AZ Quotes. Retrieved from **https://www.azquotes.com/author/7739-Khloe_Kardashian**

Lamas, L. (n.d.). *Quote on success*. AZ Quotes. Retrieved from **https://www.azquotes.com/author/56378-Lorenzo_Lamas**

Guitarist Next Door. (n.d.). *Best jazz guitarists of all time*. Retrieved from **https://guitaristnextdoor.com/best-jazz-guitarists-of-all-time/**

Best of Jazz. (n.d.). *The best jazz guitarists*. Retrieved from **https://bestofjazz.org/the-best-jazz-guitarists/**

How to apply syncopation to your guitar playing. (n.d.). *Dummies*. Retrieved from **https://www.dummies.com/article/academics-the-arts/music/instruments/guitar/how-to-apply-syncopation-to-your-guitar-playing-198057/**

WebbWell. (n.d.). *Course disclaimer*. Retrieved from **http://webbwell.com/course-disclaimer/**

GreaseMax. (n.d.). *Disclaimer*. Retrieved from **https://greasemax.au/disclaimer/**

Goodwill Car Donations. (n.d.). *Car donations*. Retrieved from **https://www.gwcars.org/faqs/accepted-vehicles/car-donations/**

Moms Who Think. (n.d.). *What you need to know about navigating perimenopause*. Retrieved from **https://www.momswhothink.com/perimenopause-symptoms/**

MusicianTuts. (n.d.). *Guitar quotes*. Retrieved from **https://musiciantuts.com/guitar-quotes/**

BrainyQuote. (n.d.). *Rhythm quotes*. BrainyQuote. Retrieved from **https://www.brainyquote.com/search_results?x=0&y=0&q=rhythm**

BrainyQuote. (n.d.). *Collaboration quotes*. BrainyQuote. Retrieved from **https://www.brainyquote.com/search_results?x=0&y=0&q=collaboration**

Thalia Capos. (n.d.). *The quotable Chet Atkins*. Retrieved from **https://www.thaliacapos.com/blogs/blog/the-quotable-chet-atkins**

BrainyQuote. (n.d.). Luke Bryan quote on country music. BrainyQuote. Retrieved from **https://www.brainyquote.com/quotes/luke_bryan_497158**

BrainyQuote. (n.d.). *Advancing quotes*. BrainyQuote. Retrieved from **https://www.brainyquote.com/search_results?x=0&y=0&q=ADVANCING**

YouTube. (2023). *[Journey To an Extraordinary Life-Tad Sisler and Louie Stevens]*. YouTube. **https://www.youtube.com/watch?v=-wYCSRDy1ic**

ScienceDaily. (2024, January 29). *Playing an instrument boosts brain's executive function, study finds*. ScienceDaily. **https://www.sciencedaily.com/releases/2024/01/240129122415.htm**

Musician Wave. (n.d.). *Guitar quotes*. Retrieved from **https://www.musicianwave.com/guitar-quotes/**

TrueFire. (n.d.). *10 quotes from rock guitarists on their passion for the guitar*. Retrieved from **https://blog.truefire.com/guitar-lessons/10-quotes-from-rock-guitarists-on-their-passion-for-the-guitar/**

GuitarHabits. (n.d.). *19 inspiring famous guitar player quotes*. Retrieved from **https://www.guitarhabits.com/19-inspiring-famous-guitar-player-quotes/**

Green Hills Guitar Studio. (n.d.). *The art of dynamics: Bringing emotion to your guitar playing*. Retrieved from **https://greenhillsguitarstudio.com/the-art-of-dynamics-bringing-emotion-to-your-guitar-playing/**

AZ Quotes. (n.d.). *Elliott Gould quotes*. AZ Quotes. **https://www.azquotes.com/author/31289-Elliott_Gould**

MODERN RENAISSANCE
PUBLISHING